THE BIG BOOK
OF PATCHWORK

7/7/12

D0886091

THE BIG BOOK
OF PATCHWORK

50 FABULOUS QUILTS
FROM JUDY HOPKINS

Martingale®
& COMPANY

DEDICATION

For the indomitable Judy Betts Morrison, who opened her shop and her heart to the quilters of Anchorage—and gave this fledgling quilt professional room to soar.

ACKNOWLEDGMENTS

Grateful thanks to the quiltmakers and the quilters and to those who loaned quilts from their collections, including those whose names have been lost in time. Your generous contributions made this book possible.

The Big Book of Patchwork: 50 Fabulous Quilts from Judy Hopkins
© 2011 by Judy D. Hopkins

That Patchwork Place® is an imprint of Martingale & Company®.

Martingale & Company
19021 120th Ave. NE, Suite 102
Bothell, WA 98011-9511
www.martingale-pub.com

CREDITS

President & CEO: Tom Wierzbicki
Editorial Director: Mary V. Green
Managing Editor: Tina Cook
Design Director: Stan Green
Developmental Editor: Karen Costello Soltys
Technical Editor: Laurie Baker
Copy Editor: Melissa Bryan
Production Manager: Regina Girard
Illustrator: Laurel Strand
Cover & Text Designer: Stan Green
Photographer: Brent Kane

MISSION STATEMENT

Dedicated to providing quality products and service to inspire creativity.

Printed in China
16 15 14 13 12 11   8 7 6 5 4 3 2 1

Library of Congress Cataloging-in-Publication Data is available upon request.

ISBN: 978-1-56477-907-6

CONTENTS

INTRODUCTION

Quilters still love making classic quilts, and there are a lot to choose from here! This enticing collection of projects includes table runners, crib quilts, nap quilts, and bed-size quilts based on traditional patterns, in a variety of eye-catching fabric and color combinations: dramatic two-fabric and two-color quilts, pleasing repeat-fabric quilts, and satisfyingly scrappy multifabric quilts. Some of the projects began life as mystery quilt patterns, but the versions in this book generally vary in some significant way from the original designs and include updated instructions, illustrations, and techniques.

Many of these quilt projects are about the size of an afghan, perfect for napping. I like making quilts this size because I can play with design, color, and fabric without investing a lot of time and money, and they're relatively easy to quilt on a home sewing machine. This is also a nice size for a gift: It can be displayed proudly if the recipient truly loves it, quietly folded up and stashed if it doesn't quite suit the giftee's tastes or new decor, and thoroughly enjoyed at nap time in either case. If you want bigger quilts, you can usually bring a nap-sized project up to queen size by making four times the number of blocks and adding one or more borders in appropriate fabrics.

I've been brief with the basic instructions in this book, to make room for as many projects as possible. Perhaps you'll want to ease into things with a simple, triangle-free project like "Log Jam" (page 101) or "Salmonberry" (page 129). See if you can make "Broken Sash" (page 37) or "Purse Seiner" (page 123) completely from your stash. Or work as my grandmother might have done, making "Lost Ship" (page 107) or "Soaring Gulls" (page 138) by using what's on hand for the smaller pieces and treating yourself to new yardage for backgrounds, setting pieces, and/or borders.

You'll see some "cousins" among the projects, too—the "Streak of Lightning" quilt (page 141) goes nicely with "Japanese Sampler" (page 93), and "Mt. Fairweather" (page 110) and "Twilight Lane" (page 147) seem to share some DNA. The "Hide and Seek" quilt (page 84) and the "Flying Geese" quilt (page 66) were deliberately made using similar colors and fabrics for the twin beds in our guest room.

Whatever your taste and mood, I'm sure you'll find more than one project you just can't wait to make. Have a fabulous time!

Broken Sash (page 37)

Purse Seiner (page 123)

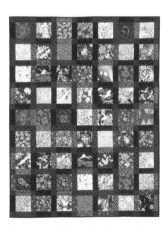

Japanese Sampler (page 93)

Streak of Lightning (page 141)

Basic Quiltmaking
Instructions

Read the complete instructions for the quilt you plan to make before you begin. You may want to make a sample block to test the pattern and confirm your fabric choices before you proceed. This also might help you avoid cutting errors and could expose piecing quirks that would be helpful to know about early in the process.

FABRIC SELECTION

When you make a quilt from a pattern book like this one, where the quilt's size, setting arrangement, and color scheme are specified, it's the fabrics you choose to work with that make your project personal and unique. Many of the quilts in this book are multi-fabric quilts that rely on runs of fabric in particular color families. The materials list, for example, might call for eight assorted cream prints and eight assorted dark green prints. Choose prints in a variety of scales and visual textures, and try not to overmatch the colors. Don't hesitate to include two-color and multicolor prints in your color runs; they often add needed liveliness to a quilt.

For the cream prints, you could choose eight different prints in light, creamy colors that range from ivory to ecru.

A cream color run

A color run in the green family might include forest greens, moss greens, emerald greens, and blue-greens. Spice up the mix by adding a small amount of an adjacent color, such as blue, and/or a neutral, such as brown or black. Neutrals can be added to any color scheme without changing it; they add interest without calling attention to themselves.

If the materials section calls for fabrics in a particular value range—such as assorted dark prints—the fabrics can be all the same color, closely related colors, or assorted colors, as long as they're all the same value. A dark color run, for instance, might include dark greens, browns, deep reds, dark blues, and black.

Visual Texture

Textural variety adds interest to repeat-fabric quilts, such as "Grandmother's Choice" (page 78.) Create more interesting quilts by combining plaids and stripes with a floral fabric, or by mixing large- or medium-scale multicolored prints with quieter tone-on-tone designs. Experiment to find combinations that appeal to you.

Two-Fabric Quilts

Several of the quilts in this book are two-fabric or two-color quilts, such as "Wagon Tracks" (page 154) and "Equinox" (page 63). The most important element in selecting fabric for these quilts is contrast—the fabric used for the design must contrast strongly with the fabric used for the background. You'll know you have sufficient contrast if you can clearly see the "line" where patches of the two fabrics are joined.

From left to right: not enough contrast, good contrast, better contrast!

A green color run

ROTARY CUTTING

The quilts in this book are all rotary cut. You'll be cutting strips from fabric and cutting squares and rectangles from some of those strips. Other strips may be joined to make strip units, which are then cut into segments.

All cutting measurements given in the pattern instructions include ¼"-wide seam allowances; don't add seam allowances to the dimensions given.

Rotary-cutting and strip-piecing techniques sometimes yield more pieces than actually are needed to make a particular block or quilt. For example, cutting all the way to the end of a strip unit without counting the number of pieces cut may give you more pieces than you need. Use any leftovers as part of a pieced back, or toss them into the scrap bag for a future quilt.

Equipment

Basic rotary-cutting tools include a medium-sized (45 mm) rotary cutter and an 18" x 24" self-healing cutting mat. You'll also need a 24"-long acrylic cutting ruler and a 6" or 8" cutting square, both marked in ⅛" increments. Smaller cutting mats and rulers in other sizes can be useful but aren't required for the projects in this book.

When a rotary blade seems dull, take your rotary cutter apart and put a small drop of sewing-machine oil on the blade; wipe both sides carefully with a soft, clean cloth. Wipe the safety guard and other parts before you reassemble the cutter. If the blade still isn't cutting cleanly through the fabric, replace it.

Keep your cutter's safety guard closed except when you're actually making a cut. Never leave a rotary cutter, open or closed, within reach of children! Dispose of used blades safely.

Cutting Strips, Squares, and Rectangles

The first step is to straighten the raw edge of the fabric. Fold the fabric in half lengthwise, aligning the selvages. Lay the fabric on the cutting mat with the fold of the fabric closest to you and the bulk of the fabric to your left (reverse the layout if you're left-handed).

Align a horizontal line of a long cutting ruler with the fold of the fabric. Cut along the edge of the ruler, through both layers of fabric.

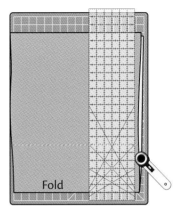

Move to the opposite side of the table, or rotate the cutting mat so the bulk of the fabric is to your right. If necessary, accordion-fold the fabric and pile it on the mat, being careful not to disturb your freshly cut edge.

Cut strips to the width given in the project instructions, measuring from the straight cut on the left. If you need a 3"-wide strip, for example, place the 3" line of the ruler on the straightened edge of the fabric. Combine a cutting square with the long ruler to make cuts wider than the long ruler allows.

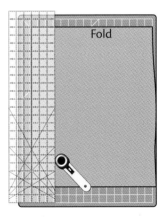

If necessary, restraighten the edge after you've made several cuts.

To cut squares and rectangles from a strip, straighten the selvage ends of the folded strip by aligning a horizontal line of a cutting square with the long edge of the folded strip; cut along the edge of the ruler through both layers, removing the selvages in the process. Rotate the mat so the clean-cut end of the strip is on the left. Align the proper measurement on your cutting square with the straightened end of the strip, and cut the fabric into squares or rectangles the width of the strip. Sometimes you can get an additional piece by unfolding the strip when you reach the right-hand edge.

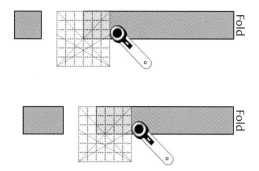

To make half-square triangles, cut squares in half diagonally. To make quarter-square triangles, cut squares into quarters diagonally, as shown.

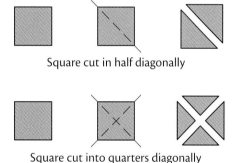

Square cut in half diagonally

Square cut into quarters diagonally

For many of the quilts in this book, you'll be making blocks and units by cutting strips of fabric, sewing the strips together in a particular order to make strip units, and then cutting the strip units into segments.

Make the strip units and press the seam allowances as described in the project instructions. Straighten the right end of each strip unit by aligning a horizontal line of a cutting square with one of the strip unit's internal seams and cutting along the edge of the ruler. Place the straightened end on the left. Align the desired measurement on your cutting square with the straightened end and cut, repeating until you have the required number of segments. If necessary, restraighten the end after you've made several cuts.

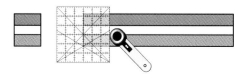

PIECING

A well-maintained straight-stitch sewing machine is adequate for most quiltmaking operations. If you're using a zigzag sewing machine, replace the zigzag throat plate with a plate that has a small round hole for the needle to pass through, one especially designed for straight stitching. Clean and oil your machine frequently.

Use sewing-machine needles properly sized for cotton fabrics and change them often; dull or bent needles can snag your fabric and can cause your machine to skip stitches. Set the stitch length at 10 to 12 stitches per inch. Make sure the tension is adjusted properly to produce smooth, even seams. Use 100% cotton thread; I use a medium greenish gray thread (the color you get when you mix all the Easter-egg dyes together) for piecing all but the lightest and darkest fabrics.

The most important skill for a quilter to master is sewing accurate ¼" seam allowances. If your seam allowance is off by even a few threads, your seams may not line up and your units and blocks may not be the desired finished size; this will affect the measurements for everything else in the quilt.

Test your seam-allowance width by cutting three short strips of fabric, each exactly 2" wide. Join the pieces into a strip unit, press the seam allowances, and measure the finished width of the center strip. If you're sewing an accurate ¼" seam allowance, the center strip will measure exactly 1½". If it doesn't, you need to adjust or compensate for whatever you're using as a seam guide, whether it's a special ¼" sewing-machine foot, a particular needle-position setting, an engraved line on your sewing machine, or simply a piece of tape you've put on your sewing-machine bed. Some quilters find they need to sew a scant ¼"—just a thread or two short of a full ¼"—to allow for take-up when seam allowances are pressed.

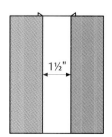

Join 2" strips and measure the center.

If your seam-width test indicates you need a seam guide other than the edge of your presser foot or a line engraved on your machine, put a strip of moleskin or several layers of masking tape along your perfect ¼" line. Make sure the tape doesn't interfere with the feed dogs.

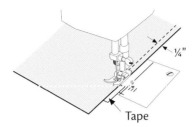

Use a hot iron on the cotton setting to gently press every seam before attaching a new piece of fabric. Some quilters use a dry iron, while others prefer steam.

I press seam allowances open to make it easier to hand stitch the allover quilting patterns I commonly use for my quilts. However, the traditional quilters' rule is to press seam allowances to one side, toward the darker fabric or toward the section with fewer seams. Side-pressed seam allowances are stronger, and it's easier for most people to make corners meet properly when they can match opposing seam allowances.

Opposing seam allowances
on wrong side of fabric

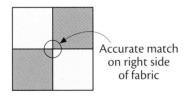

Accurate match
on right side
of fabric

Snip or pull out loose threads that have been caught in the seams as you press; it's easier to tidy up the pieces when you're pressing the individual seams than to go back over the entire quilt later.

When sewing two pieces or units together, you may need to ease excess fabric. To ease, pin the pieces together at the seams and ends—and in between,

if necessary—to distribute the excess fabric. When you stitch the seam, place the shorter piece on top. The feed dogs will help ease the fullness of the longer piece.

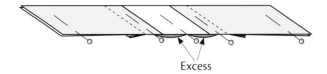

Excess

Save time and thread by chain piecing. Place the pieces that are to be joined right sides together with raw edges even; pin as necessary. When possible, arrange opposing seam allowances so the top seam allowance faces toward the needle and the lower seam allowance faces toward you. Feed the units under the presser foot one after the other, without lifting the presser foot or clipping the connecting threads; backstitching isn't necessary. Clip the threads between the pieces either before or after pressing.

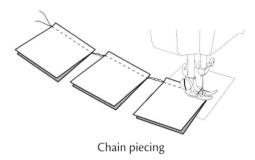

Chain piecing

It's wise to sew a complete block together before you start working in this assembly-line fashion, to ensure that the pieces have been accurately cut and to identify piecing quirks you may need to watch out for.

Use a seam ripper to remove unwanted stitching. To avoid stretching the fabric, cut the thread every four or five stitches on one side of the fabric. Pull the thread on the reverse side; it should come out easily.

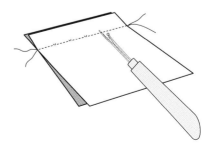

Stitching Tips for Square-in-a-Square Units

Join the opposing triangles first, centering the triangles on the square. The triangle points will be sticking out about ⅜" beyond the edges of the square. Press the seam allowances toward the triangles.

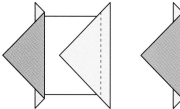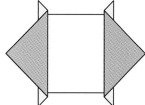

Join the remaining triangles to the square. Your ¼" seam allowance should exactly intersect the 90° angle where the two triangles meet at both the top and bottom ends of the seam, as in the magnified areas of the illustration. To accomplish this, adjust the position of the loose triangle until the seam lines up correctly at A. Take a few stitches, and then adjust the point at B and finish stitching the seam. Press the seam allowances toward the triangles.

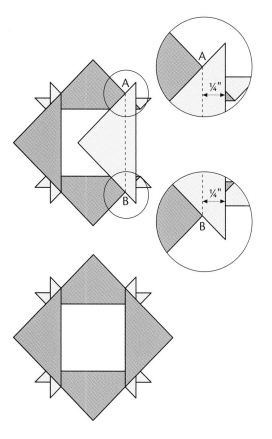

SQUARING UP BLOCKS

If your blocks become distorted during the stitching process, square them up with a freezer-paper guide. Use an accurate cutting square and a pencil or permanent pen to draw a square (finished block size plus seam allowance) on the plain side of the freezer paper. Iron the freezer paper to your ironing-board cover, plastic-coated side down. Align the block edges with the penciled lines and pin the block in place. Gently steam-press. Let each block cool before you unpin it from the freezer-paper guide.

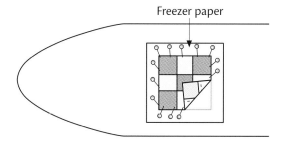

Freezer paper

SETTING THE BLOCKS TOGETHER

Straight Sets

In straight-set quilts the blocks and units are laid out with their edges parallel to the edges of the quilt. Constructing a straight-set quilt is simple and straightforward. When you set blocks side by side without sashing, simply stitch them together in horizontal rows, pressing the seam allowances in opposite directions from row to row. Sew the rows together to complete the patterned section of the quilt, matching the seams between the blocks.

If the pattern calls for alternate blocks, lay out the primary and alternate blocks in checkerboard fashion and stitch them together in rows, pressing the seam allowances toward the alternate blocks.

Straight Sets with Plain Sashing

When setting blocks together with plain sashing, cut the vertical sashing pieces the same length as the blocks (including seam allowance) and the desired finished width, plus seam allowance. Join the sashing pieces and the blocks to form rows, starting and ending each row with a block. Join the rows with long strips of the sashing fabric, cut to the same width as the shorter sashing pieces. Make sure the corners of the blocks are aligned when you stitch the rows together.

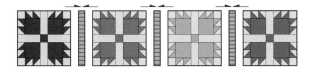

Straight Sets with Pieced Sashing

When setting blocks together with sashing pieces and sashing squares (corner squares cut from a different fabric), join the vertical sashing pieces to the blocks to form rows, beginning and ending each row with a sashing piece. Press seam allowances toward the sashing pieces. Join the sashing squares to the horizontal sashing pieces to make pieced sashing

strips, beginning and ending each row with a sashing square. Press seam allowances toward the sashing pieces. Join the rows of blocks and the pieced sashing strips.

Bar Quilts

In a bar quilt, various units are joined into rows, or bars, instead of blocks; the pattern emerges only after the bars are stitched together. Several different bar formats might be combined to form the overall pattern. Make sure the design, fabrics, and colors will come out as you intended by laying out the pieced units for several bars—or for the entire quilt—before you begin to sew.

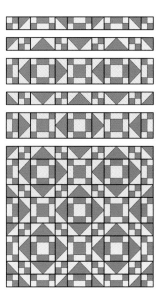

On-Point Sets

Quilts that are set on point are constructed in diagonal rows, with plain setting triangles or pieced half and quarter blocks added to complete the sides and corners of the quilt. To avoid confusion, lay out all the blocks and setting pieces in the proper configuration before you start sewing. Pick up and sew one row at a time, and then join the rows. Add the corner triangles last.

Trim and square up the outside edges after the rows are sewn, leaving ¼" outside the block points for seams. Leave more space outside the block points if the triangles have been cut large to allow the blocks to "float."

ADDING THE BORDERS

Because extra yardage is needed to cut borders on the lengthwise grain, borders for most of the quilts in this book are cut selvage to selvage and seamed as necessary to make strips long enough to border the quilt. Remove the selvages and press the seam allowances open for minimum visibility.

Measure the length of the quilt through the center, from raw edge to raw edge. Cut two border strips to this measurement and join them to the sides of the

quilt with a ¼" seam allowance, matching the ends and centers and easing the edges to fit. Press the seam allowances toward the borders.

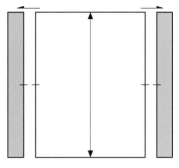

Measure center of quilt,
top to bottom. Mark centers.

Measure the width of the quilt at the center, including the border pieces you just added. Cut the remaining two border strips to this measurement and join them to the top and bottom edges of the quilt, matching ends and centers and easing as necessary. Press the seam allowances toward the borders.

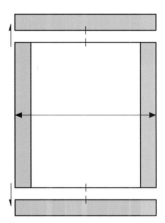

Measure center of quilt, side to side,
including border strips. Mark centers.

PREPARING THE BACKING

Yardage requirements for backings are calculated to use the least amount of fabric. For the quilts in this book, you'll cut two or three lengths of fabric from the specified yardage and join them along the long edges using a ½" seam allowance. The project instructions will tell you whether the backing seams are intended to be oriented crosswise or lengthwise in the quilt.

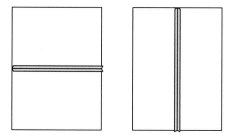

For more variety, or simply to be more frugal, piece a multi-fabric backing. Use fabric and blocks left over from piecing the front of the quilt; add other fabrics from your stash. Quilters have even been known to use quilt tops they're not particularly proud of to back quilts they like better!

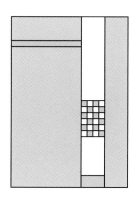

PREPARING TO QUILT

Professional quilters using long-arm quilting machines quilted many of the projects in this book. If you opt to have your quilt professionally quilted, check with your long-arm quilter before you deliver your quilt, backing, and batting—quilts don't need to be layered and basted for long-arm machine quilting, but there may be other special requirements you should be aware of.

Follow the instructions in this section if you plan to quilt by hand or on your home sewing machine.

1. Let your batting relax overnight—or toss it in the dryer and let it air-fluff for 10 minutes—before you layer your quilt.

2. Spread the backing on a large table, wrong side up, and anchor it with masking tape or binder clips. Center the batting over the backing, smoothing out any wrinkles.

3. Center the quilt top on the batting, right side up; gently smooth any fullness to the sides and corners. Keep the major horizontal and vertical seams, such as those that attach the borders to the quilt, as straight as possible.

4. For hand quilting, baste the three layers together with a long needle and light-colored thread; start in the center and work diagonally to each corner, making a large X. Continue basting, making a grid of horizontal and vertical lines no more than 6" apart. Finish by basting around the outside edges.

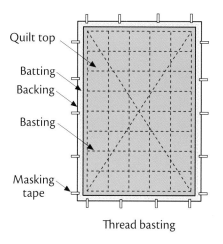

Thread basting

For machine quilting, baste the layers with No. 2 rustproof safety pins placed 3" to 4" apart. Secure the outside edges with straight pins.

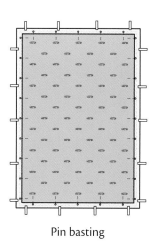

Pin basting

A quilt-tack tool can be used to baste quilts for either hand or machine quilting. The method is fast and holds the layers securely. The T-shaped tabs of the tacks are easy to remove if they get in the way of the needle.

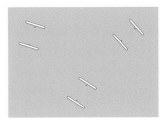

Quilt tacks

TRIMMING AND STRAIGHTENING THE QUILT

When the quilting is complete, prepare for binding by trimming and straightening the quilt. Measure from a border seam line (or from a major interior seam) to the outside edge of the quilt top in several places around the quilt. Using the smallest measurement, position a ruler along the seam line you measured from and trim the excess batting and backing from all four sides of the quilt. Use a large square ruler to square up the corners.

ATTACHING A HANGING SLEEVE

If you plan to display your finished quilt on the wall, add a hanging sleeve large enough to hold a curtain rod, a dowel, or a piece of lath. Prepare the sleeve and baste it to the top of the quilt before the binding is attached, as described below.

1. Cut a piece of fabric 6" to 8" wide by the width of the quilt, piecing if necessary. Fold the short ends under ½", then ½" again; machine hem the folded edges.

2. Fold the fabric strip in half lengthwise, wrong sides together. Center the folded strip on the back of the quilt and baste the raw edges to the top edge of the quilt, taking a scant ¼"-wide seam allowance.

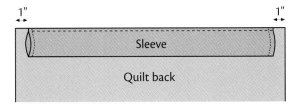

3. Bind the quilt edges as instructed in "Adding the Binding" on the facing page, enclosing the raw edges of the sleeve. After the binding has been blindstitched in place, push the top layer of the sleeve up so the top edge covers about half of the binding. This will provide a little give so the hanging rod doesn't put strain on the quilt itself. Blindstitch the bottom layer of the sleeve ends and the bottom edge of the sleeve in place, taking care not to catch the front of the quilt as you stitch.

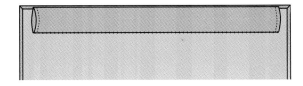

4. To hang the quilt, slide a curtain rod, wooden dowel, or piece of lath through the sleeve. The larger and heavier the quilt, the thicker and sturdier the hanging rod must be. Cut the dowel or lath the width of the quilt top minus 1". Hang the quilt by resting the rod or dowel on two flat-head nails. If you're using lath, attach screw eyes or drill holes at each end, and slip the holes or eyes over small, flathead nails.

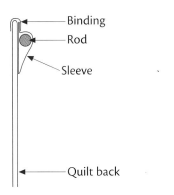

ADDING THE BINDING

Fabric requirements for bindings assume ⅜"-wide (finished), double-fold binding, made from straight-grain strips cut 2½" wide and stitched to the outside edges of the quilt with a ⅜"-wide seam allowance. You'll need enough binding to go around the perimeter of the quilt plus about 18".

Remove the selvages from the binding strips and join the ends to make one long, continuous strip. Press the seam allowances open, and then press the strip in half lengthwise, wrong sides together.

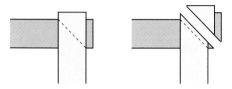

Joining straight-cut strips

Place the binding on the front of the quilt about 15" from a corner, lining up the raw edges of the binding with the raw edges of the quilt. Using a walking foot, sew the binding to the quilt with a ⅜"-wide seam allowance; leave the first 6" of binding loose so you can more easily join the beginning and the end of the binding strip later.

End the line of stitching ⅜" from the corner of the quilt; backstitch.

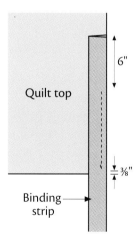

Remove the quilt from the machine and prepare for sewing along the next edge. Fold the binding strip away from the quilt at a 45° angle, and then fold it back on itself, keeping the raw edge even with the next edge of the quilt. There will be an angled fold at the corner; the second, straight fold should be even with the top edge of the quilt. Beginning ⅜" from the edge of the straight fold, stitch to ⅜" from the next corner, keeping the binding aligned with the raw edge of the quilt.

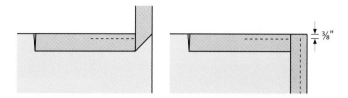

Fold the binding away from the quilt as you did at the previous corner and continue around the edge of the quilt, repeating the same procedure at the remaining corners. Approximately 10" from the starting point, stop and backstitch. Leave a 6" tail.

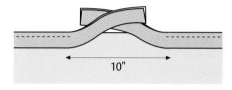

Fold the unstitched binding edges back on themselves so that they meet in the middle over the unsewn area of the quilt edge. Press the folds.

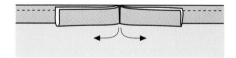

Unfold both ends of the binding. Lay the ending strip flat, right side up. Lay the beginning strip over it, right side down, matching the centers of the pressed Xs. Carefully draw a diagonal line through the point where the fold lines meet. Pin, and then stitch on the marked line.

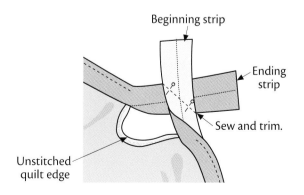

Check to make sure the newly seamed binding fits the unbound edge. Trim off the tail ends ¼" from the seam; press the seam allowances open. Refold the binding, press the fold, and stitch the remainder of the binding to the quilt edge.

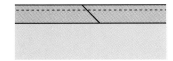

Fold the binding to the back over the raw edges of the quilt. The folded edge of the binding should just cover the stitching line. Blindstitch the binding in place, making sure your stitches don't go through to the front of the quilt. Blindstitch the folds in the miters that form at each corner, if you wish.

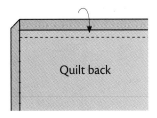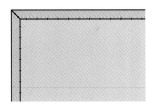

MAKING A LABEL

Be sure to sign and date your work! At the very least, embroider your name and the year you completed the quilt on the front or back of the quilt, or incorporate this information in the quilting. One quilter I know uses her sewing machine's alphabet and number functions to stitch her name and the date on short lengths of grosgrain ribbon. She places these little labels at an angle in the bottom back corners of the quilt and secures the ends when she whips down the binding.

Future generations will want to know more than just the "who" and "when." With today's tools, it's easy to make an attractive and informative label to blindstitch to the back of your quilt. Include the name of the quilt, the maker's name, the quilter's name (if different from the maker), the city and state in which the quilt was made, the date, whom the quilt was made for and why, and any other interesting or important information about the quilt. For an antique quilt, record everything you know about the quilt, including where you purchased it.

Write the information on a piece of fabric with a reliable permanent marker, like a Pigma Micron pen. Use colored markers and add little drawings for a fancier result. Press a piece of plastic-coated freezer paper to the wrong side of your label fabric to stabilize it while you write or draw. You can draw lines on the plain side of the freezer paper with a wide-tipped marker to help you keep your writing straight.

If you have the equipment and the expertise, you can print fabric labels on a laser printer or with a photocopier. Computer printers and photocopiers that can handle index-weight paper usually can process a sheet of stabilized fabric. Iron a 9" x 12" piece of freezer paper to the back of a 9" x 12" piece of fabric, then trim this paper-and-fabric sandwich to 8½" x 11". Design your label, and then print it on the fabric. Let the label stand for a few hours after it emerges from the printer or copier, and then heat-set it by pressing with a hot, dry iron. Use a pressing cloth and let the iron remain on each section of the label for at least 30 seconds.

Always test to be absolutely sure the ink used for your label is permanent. Be aware that labels that safely pass the washing-machine test sometimes bleed when they're dry-cleaned. Both handwritten and printed labels may fade with time or after repeated washings.

ALASKA WILDFLOWERS

Pieced by Beverly Fugazzi; quilted by Lisa Cavanaugh

Finished block: 12" x 12"
Finished quilt: 51" x 64"

MATERIALS

Yardage is based on 42"-wide fabric.

1⅓ yards of dark purple print for sashing and outer border*

½ yard of yellow print for inner border*

16 rectangles, 9" x 17", of assorted purple prints for blocks. Use darks and dark-mediums that range from red-violet to blue-violet.**

12 rectangles, 9" x 17", of assorted yellow prints for blocks**

1½" x 32" strip of lime green print for sashing posts

⅝ yard of medium purple print for binding*

3½ yards of fabric for backing

57" x 70" piece of batting

Use one of the block fabrics or a completely different fabric.

**Use the same fabric more than once, if you wish.*

CUTTING

All cutting dimensions include ¼"-wide seam allowances. **Note:** *You may want to wait until your blocks are pieced before cutting sashing strips, in case your blocks measure larger or smaller than the expected 12½" x 12½" (raw edge to raw edge).*

From *each* of the 12 assorted yellow prints, cut:
1 strip, 2⅞" x 17" (12 total); crosscut *each* strip into 4 squares, 2⅞" x 2⅞" (48 total)
2 strips, 2½" x 17" (24 total)

From *each* of the 16 assorted purple prints, cut:
1 strip, 2⅞" x 17" (16 total); crosscut *each* strip into 3 squares, 2⅞" x 2⅞" (48 total)
2 strips, 2½" x 17" (32 total)

From the dark purple print, cut:
11 strips, 1½" x 42"; crosscut into 31 sashing strips, 1½" x 12½"
6 border strips, 4½" x 42"

From the lime green strip, cut:
20 sashing squares, 1½" x 1½"

From the yellow print, cut:
6 border strips, 2" x 42"

From the medium purple print, cut:
7 binding strips

MAKING THE BLOCKS

For ease of construction, press seam allowances open.

1. Layer each 2⅞" yellow square with a 2⅞" purple square, right sides together. Use as many different yellow-and-purple fabric combinations as possible. Draw a diagonal line from corner to corner on each pair of layered squares. Stitch ¼" from each side of the drawn lines. Cut on the drawn lines to make 96 half-square-triangle units.

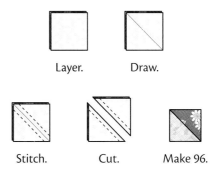

Layer.   Draw.

Stitch.   Cut.   Make 96.

2. Randomly join the 2½" x 17" strips into pairs to make 16 purple strip units and 12 yellow strip units as shown. Cut the number of 2½"-wide segments indicated.

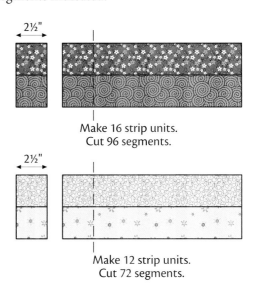

2½"

Make 16 strip units.
Cut 96 segments.

2½"

Make 12 strip units.
Cut 72 segments.

3. Randomly join the units from step 1 and 48 of the yellow strip-unit segments to make 48 unit A.

Unit A.
Make 48.

4. Randomly join the remaining strip-unit segments to make 12 unit B and 48 unit C.

Unit B.   Unit C.
Make 12.   Make 48.

5. Randomly join the A, B, and C units to make 12 Alaska Wildflower blocks.

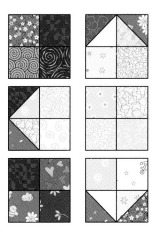 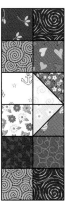

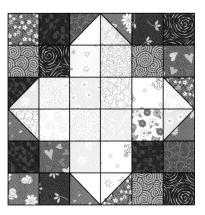

Make 12.

ASSEMBLING AND FINISHING THE QUILT

Basic instructions for borders, backing, and binding begin on page 14.

1. Join the blocks and 16 of the 1½" x 12½" dark purple sashing strips to make four block rows. Press the seam allowances toward the sashing strips.

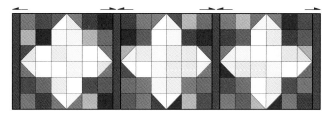

Make 4 block rows.

2. Join the remaining dark purple sashing strips and the 1½" lime green squares to make five sashing rows. Press the seam allowances toward the sashing strips.

Make 5 sashing rows.

3. Set the block rows and sashing rows together as shown in the photo on page 19.
4. Add the inner border using the 2"-wide yellow strips.
5. Add the outer border using the 4½"-wide dark purple strips.
6. Seam the backing fabric. The seam will run crosswise of the quilt.
7. Layer the quilt top with batting and backing; baste.
8. Hand or machine quilt.
9. Bind the quilt with the medium purple strips.

AUNT NANCY'S FAVORITE

Pieced by Dianna "Dee" Morrow; quilted by Bobbi Moore

Finished block: 12" x 12"
Finished quilt: 66½" x 78½"

MATERIALS

Yardage is based on 42"-wide fabric.

2½ yards of multicolored focal print for border
10 strips, 7½" x 42", of assorted dark prints for blocks. Use rusts, teals, taupes, and grays.
10 strips, 5½" x 42", of assorted medium prints for blocks. Use peaches, aquas, and medium taupes and grays.
10 strips, 7½" x 42", of assorted light prints that coordinate with the dark and medium prints for blocks
⅔ yard of dark fabric for binding
5¼ yards of fabric for backing
73" x 85" piece of batting

CUTTING

All cutting dimensions include ¼"-wide seam allowances.

From *each* of the 10 assorted light print strips, cut:
1 square, 7¼" x 7¼" (10 total); cut the squares into quarters diagonally to make 40 triangles
2 rectangles, 3⅞" x 8½" (20 total)
4 rectangles, 2⅝" x 4¾" (40 total)

From *each* of the 10 assorted dark print strips, cut:
1 square, 7¼" x 7¼" (10 total); cut the squares into quarters diagonally to make 40 triangles
1 square, 4¾" x 4¾" (10 total)
2 squares, 4¼" x 4¼" (20 total); cut the squares into quarters diagonally to make 80 triangles
1 rectangle, 3⅞" x 8½" (10 total)

From *each* of the 10 assorted medium print strips, cut:
1 square, 4¾" x 4¾" (10 total)
2 squares, 4¼" x 4¼" (20 total); cut the squares into quarters diagonally to make 80 triangles
1 rectangle, 3⅞" x 8½" (10 total)
4 rectangles, 2⅝" x 4¾" (40 total)

From the focal print, cut:
8 border strips, 9¾" x 42"

From the dark fabric for binding, cut:
8 strips

MAKING THE BLOCKS

For ease of construction, press seam allowances open.

1. Layer each 3⅞" x 8½" dark print rectangle with a 3⅞" x 8½" light print rectangle, right sides together, to make 10 contrasting strip pairs. Cut two squares, 3⅞" x 3⅞", from each strip pair (20 total). Cut the layered squares in half diagonally. Do not separate the triangle pairs.

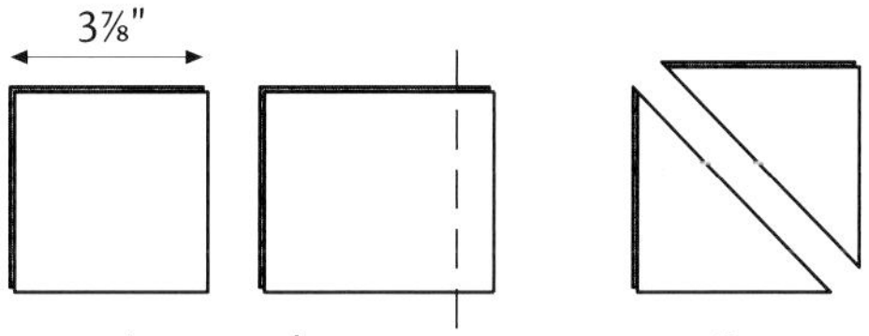

Layer and cut. Cut.

2. Chain stitch the triangle pairs along the long edges to make 40 light/dark half-square-triangle units.

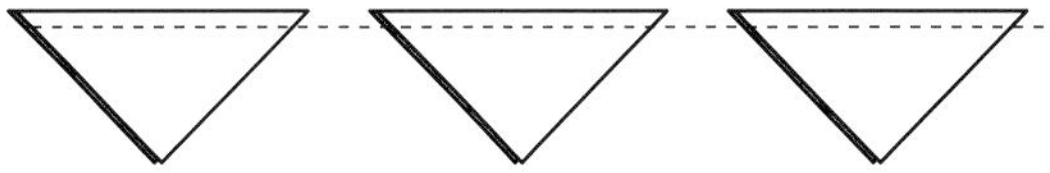

Stitch.

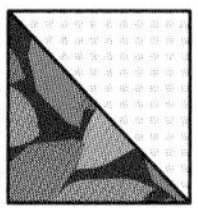

Make 40.

3. Repeat steps 1 and 2 with the remaining 3⅞" x 8½" light print rectangles and the 3⅞" x 8½" medium print rectangles to make 40 light/medium half-square-triangle units.

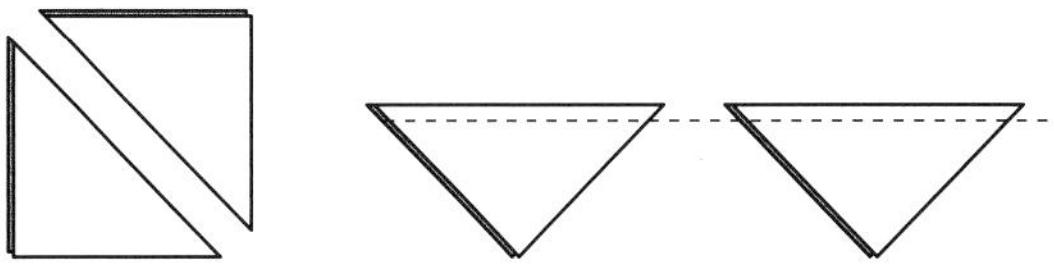

Cut. Stitch.

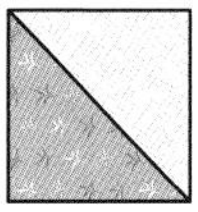

Make 40.

4. Join four identical light/dark half-square-triangle units and eight identical 4¼" medium print triangles to make four unit A. Repeat with the remaining light/dark half-square-triangle units and 4¼" medium print triangles to make 10 sets, each consisting of four matching A units.

Unit A.
Make 10 sets of
4 matching units.

5. Repeat step 4 with the light/medium half-square-triangle units and the 4¼" dark print triangles to make 10 sets of four matching B units.

Unit B.
Make 10 sets of
4 matching units.

6. Join a 2⅝" x 4¾" light rectangle to each unit A to make 10 sets of four matching C units, and then join a 2⅝" x 4¾" medium rectangle to each unit B to make 10 sets of four matching D units. **Note:** In the C units, the light rectangles should be *different from* the light triangles.

Unit C.
Make 10 sets of
4 matching units.

Unit D.
Make 10 sets of
4 matching units.

7. To each set of C units, join four matching 7¼" dark triangles and one 4¾" medium square to make block A. **Note:** In each block, the large dark triangles should be *different from* the smaller dark triangles in that block.

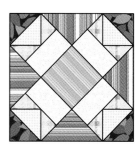
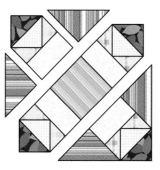

Block A.
Make 10.

8. To each set of D units, join four matching 7¼" light triangles and one 4¾" dark square to make block B. **Note:** In each block, the large light triangles should be *different from* the smaller light triangles in that block.

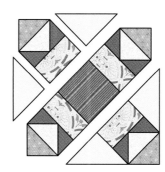
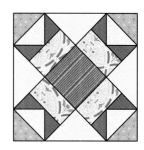

Block B.
Make 10.

ASSEMBLING AND FINISHING THE QUILT

Basic instructions for borders, backing, and binding begin on page 14.

1. Set the blocks together as shown in the photo on page 22, alternating block A and block B. Press the seam allowances in opposite directions from row to row.
2. Add the border using the 9¾"-wide focal print strips.
3. Seam the backing fabric. The seam will run lengthwise of the quilt.
4. Layer the quilt top with batting and backing; baste.
5. Hand or machine quilt.
6. Bind the quilt with the dark strips.

BEAR'S PAW

Pieced and quilted by Julie Wilkinson Kimberlin

Finished block: 10½" x 10½"
Finished quilt: 61¾" x 85¼"

MATERIALS

Yardage is based on 42"-wide fabric.

3¼ yards of striped fabric for sashing, inner and outer borders, and binding

2 yards of coral print for block backgrounds

⅓ yard of rust print for middle border

24 strips, 6¼" x about 21", of assorted medium and dark prints in browns, rusts, and taupes for blocks*

5⅝ yards of fabric for backing

68" x 92" piece of batting

Use the same fabric more than once, if you wish.

CUTTING

All cutting dimensions include ¼"-wide seam allowances. **Note:** *You may want to wait until your blocks are pieced before cutting sashing pieces, in case your blocks measure larger or smaller than the expected 11" x 11" (raw edge to raw edge).*

From *each* of the 24 assorted medium and dark prints, cut:

1 strip, 2⅜" x about 21" (24 total)

4 squares, 3½" x 3½" (96 total)

1 square, 2" x 2" (24 total)

From the coral print, cut:

12 strips, 2⅜" x 42"; cut each strip in half widthwise to make 24 strips, 2⅜" x about 21"

5 strips, 5" x 42"; crosscut into 96 rectangles, 2" x 5"

5 strips, 2" x 42"; crosscut into 96 squares, 2" x 2"

From the striped fabric, cut:

20 strips, 1¾" x 42"; crosscut 6 *strips* into 18 sashing pieces, 1¾" x 11". Leave the remaining strips uncut.

8 border strips, 6½" x 42"

8 binding strips

From the rust print, cut:

7 border strips, 1¼" x 42"

MAKING THE BLOCKS

Press the seam allowances in the direction of the arrows. If there are no arrows, press the seam allowances however you wish. **Note:** Because there are so many different fabric combinations, strip-piecing methods are not efficient for this quilt. You'll be composing and making one block at a time using just two fabrics in each block.

1. Layer a 2⅜"-wide medium or dark print strip with a 2⅜"-wide coral strip, right sides together, to make a contrasting strip pair. From this strip pair, cut eight squares, 2⅜" x 2⅜". Cut the layered squares in half diagonally. Do not separate the triangle pairs.

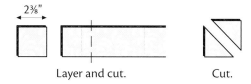

Layer and cut.   Cut.

2. Chain stitch the triangle pairs along the long edges to make 16 half-square-triangle units.

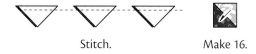

Stitch.   Make 16.

3. Join the half-square-triangle units and the 2" coral squares to make four unit A and four unit B.

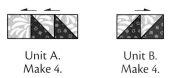

Unit A.   Unit B.
Make 4.   Make 4.

4. Join the units from step 3 with matching 3½" medium or dark squares to make four unit C.

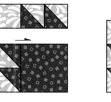

Unit C.
Make 4.

5. Join the C units with a matching 2" medium or dark square and four 2" x 5" coral rectangles to make a Bear's Paw block.

Make 1.

6. Repeat steps 1–5 with the remaining fabrics to make a total of 24 blocks.

ASSEMBLING AND FINISHING THE QUILT

Basic instructions for borders, backing, and binding begin on page 14.

1. Set the blocks together in six rows, each containing four blocks and three 1¾" x 11" striped sashing pieces, as shown below. Press the seam allowances toward the sashing pieces.

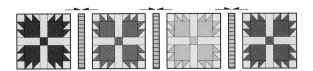

2. Join six of the 1¾" x 42" striped strips end to end, and press the seam allowances open. From this pieced strip, cut five sashing strips to the length of the block-and-sashing rows you made in step 1. Set the block rows and the sashing strips together as shown. Press the seam allowances toward the sashing strips.

3. Add the inner border using the remaining 1¾"-wide striped strips.

4. Add the middle border using the 1¼"-wide rust strips.

5. Add the outer border using the 6½"-wide striped strips.

6. Seam the backing fabric. The seam will run lengthwise of the quilt.

7. Layer the quilt top with batting and backing; baste.

8. Hand or machine quilt.

9. Bind the quilt with the striped strips.

BIRCH BRANCHES

Pieced by Janet Strait Gorton; quilted by Norma Kindred

Finished block: 10" x 10"
Finished quilt: 60" x 80"

MATERIALS

Yardage is based on 42"-wide fabric.

3 yards of dark green print for blocks, border, and binding

1 yard of white-on-white print for blocks

⅜ yard *each* of 5 assorted red prints for blocks

5 fat quarters (18" x 20") of assorted medium green prints for blocks

5 strips, 2½" x 42", of assorted light prints for blocks

4⅛ yards of fabric for backing

66" x 86" piece of batting

CUTTING

All cutting dimensions include ¼"-wide seam allowances.

From the white-on-white print, cut:
21 strips, 1½" x 42"

From the dark green print, cut:
21 strips, 1½" x 42"
8 border strips, 5½" x 42"
8 binding strips

From *each* of the 5 assorted medium green fat quarters, cut:
2 strips, 4⅞" x 20" (10 total); crosscut into 35 squares, 4⅞" x 4⅞". Cut the squares in half diagonally to make 70 triangles.
2 strips, 2⅞" x 20" (10 total); crosscut into 70 squares, 2⅞" x 2⅞". Cut the squares in half diagonally to make 140 triangles.

From *each* of the 5 assorted red prints, cut:
1 strip, 4⅞" x 42" (5 total); crosscut into:
    35 squares, 4⅞" x 4⅞"; cut in half diagonally to make 70 large triangles
    5 squares, 2⅞" x 2⅞"; cut in half diagonally to make 10 small triangles
1 strip, 2⅞" x 42" (5 total); crosscut into 65 squares, 2⅞" x 2⅞". Cut the squares in half diagonally to make 130 triangles.
1 strip, 2½" x 42" (5 total); crosscut into 70 squares, 2½" x 2½"

From *each* of the 5 assorted light strips, cut:
14 squares, 2½" x 2½" (70 total)

MAKING THE BLOCKS

Press the seam allowances in the direction of the arrows. To avoid having to twist seam allowances on the back to make them butt together properly, you'll press some of them open (as indicated by double-headed arrows).

1. Join each 1½"-wide white-on-white strip to a 1½"-wide dark green strip to make 21 strip units. From *three* of these strip units, cut 70 segments, 1½" wide. From the remaining strip units, cut 140 segments, 4½" wide.

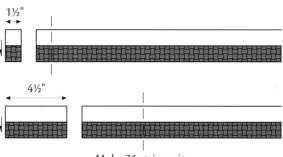

Make 21 strip units.
Cut 70 segments, 1½" wide, from 3 units.
Cut 140 segments, 4½" wide, from 18 remaining units.

2. Join the 1½"-wide strip-unit segments to make 35 unit A.

Unit A.
Make 35.

3. Join 4½"-wide strip-unit segments to opposite sides of each unit A to make 35 unit B.

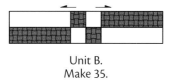

Unit B.
Make 35.

4. Randomly join 2⅞" medium green triangles to 2½" red squares to make 70 unit C.

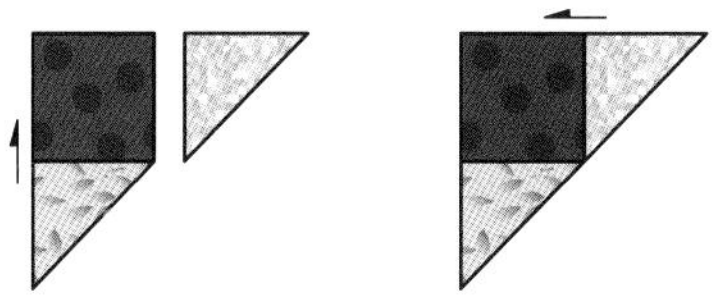

Unit C.
Make 70.

5. Randomly join 2⅞" red triangles to 2½" light squares to make 70 unit D.

Unit D.
Make 70.

6. Randomly join 4⅞" red triangles to the C units and 4⅞" medium green triangles to the D units to make 70 unit E and 70 unit F.

Unit E.
Make 70.
Unit F.
Make 70.

7. Join the remaining 4½"-wide strip-unit segments and units B, E, and F to make 35 Birch Branches blocks using two unit E and two unit F in each block. Pay particular attention to the orientation of the strip-unit segments.

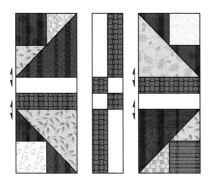

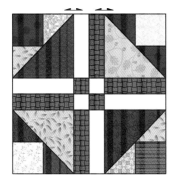

Make 35.

ASSEMBLING AND FINISHING THE QUILT

Basic instructions for borders, backing, and binding begin on page 14.

1. Set the blocks together as shown below. Note that the blocks are oriented with the red squares at the upper left and lower right. Press the seam allowances in opposite directions from row to row.

2. Add the border using the 5½"-wide dark green strips.
3. Seam the backing fabric. The seam will run lengthwise of the quilt.
4. Layer the quilt top with batting and backing; baste.
5. Hand or machine quilt.
6. Bind the quilt with the dark green strips.

BLACK SPRUCE

Pieced by Kristi Castanette; quilted by Lisa Cavanaugh

Finished block: 7½" x 7½"
Finished quilt: 19" x 71½"

MATERIALS

Yardage is based on 42"-wide fabric.

1¼ yards of multicolored focal print for outer border and binding

½ yard of red print 1 for blocks and inner border

10" x 16" rectangle of red print 2 for blocks

⅜ yard of light print for block backgrounds

⅜ yard of green print for blocks

1⅝ yards of fabric for backing

25" x 78" piece of batting

CUTTING

All cutting dimensions include ¼"-wide seam allowances.

From red print 1, cut:
2 strips, 1¾" x 42"; crosscut into:
    24 squares, 1¾" x 1¾"
    8 rectangles, 1¾" x 3"
5 border strips, 1¾" x 42"

From the rectangle of red print 2, cut:
1 strip, 3" x 16"; crosscut into 8 rectangles, 1¾" x 3"
3 strips, 1¾" x 16"; crosscut into 24 squares, 1¾" x 1¾"

From the green print, cut:
1 strip, 3¾" x 42". From *one end* of this strip, cut 2 squares, 3¾" x 3¾". Cut the squares into quarters diagonally to make 8 triangles. Pin a note that says "3¾" to these triangles. From the *remaining piece* of the 3¾" strip, cut 8 squares, 3⅜" x 3⅜". Cut these squares in half diagonally to make 16 triangles. Pin a note that says "3⅜" to these triangles.
1 strip, 3⅜" x 42"
2 strips, 1¾" x 42"; crosscut into 24 rectangles, 1¾" x 3"

From the light print, cut:
1 strip, 4⅝" x 42"; crosscut into 8 squares, 4⅝" x 4⅝". Cut the squares in half diagonally to make 16 triangles.
1 strip, 3⅜" x 42"
1 strip, 3" x 42"; crosscut into 16 rectangles, 1¾" x 3"

From the focal print, cut:
5 border strips, 5" x 42"
5 binding strips

MAKING THE BLOCKS

Press the seam allowances in the direction of the arrows. If there are no arrows, press the seam allowances however you wish.

1. Align a 1¾" square of red print 1 with the left-hand corner of each 1¾" x 3" green rectangle, right sides together. Draw a diagonal line from corner to corner on each red square as shown and stitch on the lines. Trim to leave ¼"-wide seam allowances; press.

Stitch.　　Trim.　　Make 24.

2. Align a 1¾" square of red print 2 with the right-hand corner of each unit from step 1, right sides together. Draw, stitch, trim, and press as before.

Stitch.　　Trim.　　Make 24.

3. Join 16 of the units from step 2, the 3⅜" green triangles, and the 3¾" green triangles to make eight unit A.

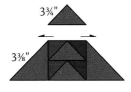

3¾"

3⅜"

Unit A.
Make 8.

4. Join 4⅝" light print triangles to the A units to make eight unit B.

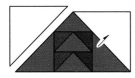 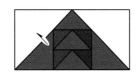

Unit B.
Make 8.

5. Join the remaining units from step 2 and the 1¾" x 3" rectangles of red prints 1 and 2 to make eight unit C. Pay particular attention to the orientation of the red 1 and red 2 rectangles.

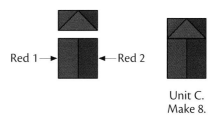

Red 1 →　　← Red 2

Unit C.
Make 8.

6. Layer the 3⅜"-wide light strip with the 3⅜"-wide green strip, right sides together. From this strip pair, cut eight squares, 3⅜" x 3⅜". Cut the layered squares in half diagonally. Do not separate the triangle pairs.

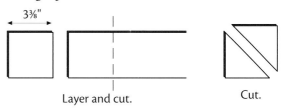

3⅜"

Layer and cut.　　Cut.

7. Chain stitch the triangle pairs along the long edges to make 16 half-square-triangle units.

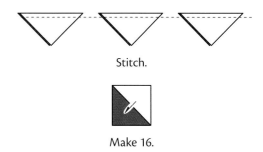

Stitch.

Make 16.

8. Join the C units, the units from step 7, and the 1¾" x 3" light rectangles to make eight unit D.

  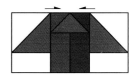

Unit D.
Make 8.

9. Join the B and D units to make eight Black Spruce blocks.

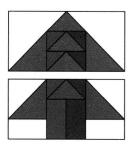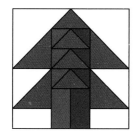

Make 8.

ASSEMBLING AND FINISHING THE QUILT

Basic instructions for borders, backing, and binding begin on page 14.

1. Set the blocks together as shown. Note that the blocks are oriented so the tree tops all point toward the center of the quilt.

2. Add the inner border using the 1¾"-wide red print 1 strips.

3. Add the outer border using the 5"-wide focal print strips.

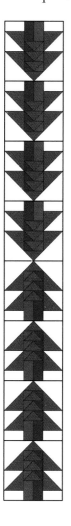

4. Seam the backing fabric. The seam will run crosswise of the quilt.

5. Layer the quilt top with batting and backing; baste.

6. Hand or machine quilt.

7. Bind the quilt with the focal print strips.

BLUEBELL

Pieced and quilted by Lisa Cavanaugh

Finished block: 6" x 6"

Finished quilt: 50" x 50"

MATERIALS

Yardage is based on 42"-wide fabric.

2⅞ yards of light yellow print for block backgrounds, fourth border, and binding

½ yard of green print for blocks

½ yard of red-violet print for third border*

¼ yard of yellow print for blocks and second border (don't use a fat quarter)

¼ yard of blue print for first border*

6 strips, 6" x 21", of assorted blue, blue-violet, purple, and red-violet prints for blocks

3½ yards of fabric for backing

56" x 56" piece of batting

Use one of the fabrics you used for the blocks or a completely different fabric.

CUTTING

All cutting dimensions include ¼"-wide seam allowances.

From the light yellow print, cut:

6 border strips, 4¾" x 42"

3 strips, 2⅞" x 42"; cut each strip in half widthwise to make 6 strips, 2⅞" x 21"

14 strips, 2½" x 42"; crosscut into:

   36 rectangles, 1½" x 2½"

   36 squares, 2½" x 2½"

   72 rectangles, 2½" x 4½"

2 strips, 1½" x 42"

6 binding strips

From *each* of the 6 assorted prints, cut:

1 strip, 2⅞" x 21" (6 total)

1 strip, 2½" x 21" (6 total); crosscut *each* strip into 6 squares, 2½" x 2½" (36 total)

From the yellow print, cut:

2 strips, 1½" x 42"

4 border strips, ¾" x 42"

From the green print, cut:

5 strips, 2½" x 42"; crosscut into 72 squares, 2½" x 2½"

From the blue print, cut:

4 border strips, 1" x 42"

From the red-violet print, cut:

5 border strips, 2½" x 42"

MAKING THE BLOCKS

For ease of construction, press the seam allowances open.

1. Join each 1½"-wide light yellow strip to a 1½"-wide yellow print strip to make two strip units. From these strip units, cut 36 segments, 1½" wide.

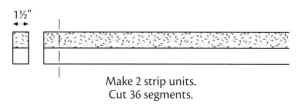

Make 2 strip units.
Cut 36 segments.

2. Join the segments from step 1 and the 1½" x 2½" light yellow rectangles to make 36 unit A.

Unit A.
Make 36.

3. Layer each 2⅞"-wide light yellow strip with a 2⅞"-wide assorted print strip, right sides together, to make six contrasting strip pairs. From *each* strip pair, cut six squares, 2⅞" x 2⅞" (36 total). Cut the layered squares in half diagonally. Do not separate the triangle pairs.

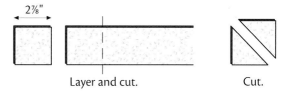

Layer and cut.   Cut.

4. Chain stitch the triangle pairs along the long edges to make 72 half-square-triangle units.

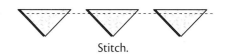

Stitch.   Make 72.

5. Join the units from steps 2 and 4 and the 2½" assorted print squares to make 36 unit B and 36 unit C *exactly* as shown. Match the assorted prints in each unit C.

Unit B.
Make 36.   Unit C.
                  Make 36.

6. Join the units from step 5 to make 36 unit D, matching the assorted prints in each unit.

Unit D.
Make 36.

7. Align 2½" green squares with the left-hand corners of 36 of the 2½" x 4½" light yellow rectangles, right sides together. Draw a diagonal line from corner to corner on each green square as shown and stitch on the lines to make 36 of unit E. Trim to leave ¼"-wide seam allowances; press.

Stitch.   Trim.   Unit E.
                                Make 36.

8. Align the remaining 2½" green squares with the left-hand corners of the remaining 2½" x 4½" light yellow rectangles, right sides together. Paying careful attention to the direction of the line, draw a diagonal line from corner to corner on each square as shown. Stitch, trim, and press as before to make 36 unit F.

Stitch.   Trim.   Unit F.
                                Make 36.

SAVE THE CORNERS
Seam the cut-off corners and use the resulting half-square-triangle units as part of a sawtooth border or for another project.

9. Join a 2½" light yellow square to each unit F to make 36 unit G.

Unit G.
Make 36.

10. Join the D, E, and G units to make 36 Bluebell blocks.

 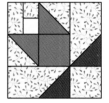

Make 36.

ASSEMBLING AND FINISHING THE QUILT

Basic instructions for borders, backing, and binding begin on page 14.

1. Set the blocks together as shown in the photo on page 34. Note that the blocks are oriented so they appear to radiate from the center of the quilt. Press the seam allowances in opposite directions from row to row.
2. Add the first border using the 1"-wide blue strips.
3. Add the second border using the ¾"-wide yellow print strips.
4. Add the third border using the 2½"-wide red-violet strips.
5. Add the fourth border using the 4¾"-wide light yellow strips.
6. Seam the backing fabric. The seam can run lengthwise or crosswise of the quilt.
7. Layer the quilt top with batting and backing; baste.
8. Hand or machine quilt.
9. Bind the quilt with the light yellow strips.

BROKEN SASH

Pieced and quilted by Julie Wilkinson Kimberlin

Finished block: 7½" x 7½"
Finished quilt: 48½" x 63½"

MATERIALS

Yardage is based on 42"-wide fabric.

1⅔ yards of multicolored print for border and binding

35 strips, exactly 4¼" x at least 18", of assorted prints for block corners*

35 squares, exactly 8" x 8", of assorted prints for block centers*

3⅓ yards of fabric for backing

55" x 70" piece of batting

Use the same fabric more than once, if you wish.

CUTTING

All cutting dimensions include ¼"-wide seam allowances.

From *each* of the 4¼" x 18" strips, cut:
4 squares, 4¼" x 4¼" (140 total)

From the multicolored print, cut:
6 border strips, 6" x 42"
7 binding strips

MAKING THE BLOCKS

Press the seam allowances in the direction of the arrows. **Note:** You'll be composing and making one block at a time, using just two fabrics in each block.

1. Choose one 8" square and four identical 4¼" squares that look good with it. Align 4¼" squares with the upper-left and lower-right corners of the 8" square, right sides together. Draw a diagonal line from corner to corner on each of the small squares as shown and stitch on the lines. Trim to leave ¼"-wide seam allowances; press.

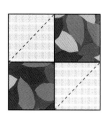   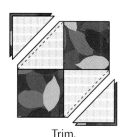

Stitch.   Trim.

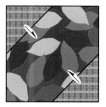

Press.

2. Align the remaining 4¼" squares with the upper-right and lower-left corners of the unit from step 1, right sides together. Draw diagonal lines from corner to corner as shown. Stitch, trim, and press as before.

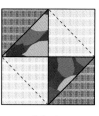   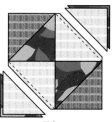

Stitch.   Trim.

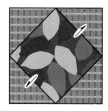

Press.

SAVE THE CORNERS

Seam the cut-off corners and use the resulting half-square-triangle units as part of a sawtooth border or for another project.

3. Repeat steps 1 and 2 with the remaining large and small squares to make a total of 35 Broken Sash blocks.

ASSEMBLING AND FINISHING THE QUILT

Basic instructions for borders, backing, and binding begin on page 14.

1. Set the blocks together as shown in the photo on page 37. Press the seam allowances in opposite directions from row to row.
2. Add the border using the 6"-wide multicolored print strips.
3. Seam the backing fabric. The seam will run crosswise of the quilt.
4. Layer the quilt top with batting and backing; baste.
5. Hand or machine quilt.
6. Bind the quilt with the multicolored print strips.

CHICKADEE QUADRILLE

Pieced by Martha M. Morris; quilted by Judy Morley

Finished block: 11¼" x 11¼"
Finished quilt: 60¾" x 76⅝"

MATERIALS

Yardage is based on 42"-wide fabric.

3¾ yards of floral print for block backgrounds and setting pieces

2⅛ yards of bright blue print for blocks, outer border, and binding

1 yard of green print for blocks and middle border

⅓ yard of pink print for blocks and inner border

5⅛ yards of fabric for backing

67" x 82" piece of batting

CUTTING

All cutting dimensions include ¼"-wide seam allowances. **Note:** *You may want to wait until your blocks are pieced before cutting the setting squares, in case your blocks measure larger or smaller than the expected 11¼" x 11¼" (raw edge to raw edge). The setting triangles are cut to a size that allows the blocks to "float."*

From the floral print, cut:

5 strips, 3¾" x 42"

4 strips, 3" x 42"; crosscut into 48 squares, 3" x 3"

7 strips, 1¾" x 42"; crosscut into 48 rectangles, 1¾" x 5½"

2 strips, 11¼" x 42"; crosscut into 6 setting squares, 11¼" x 11¼"

3 squares, 20" x 20"; cut the squares into quarters diagonally to make 12 side setting triangles (you'll use 10)

2 squares, 13¾" x 13¾"; cut the squares in half diagonally to make 4 corner setting triangles

From the bright blue print, cut:

5 strips, 3¾" x 42"

8 border strips, 3½" x 42"

8 binding strips

From the green print, cut:

4 strips, 3" x 42"; crosscut into 48 squares, 3" x 3"

7 border strips, 2½" x 42"

From the pink print, cut:

1 strip, 1¾" x 42"; crosscut into 12 squares, 1¾" x 1¾"

7 border strips, 1" x 42"

MAKING THE BLOCKS

Press the seam allowances in the direction of the arrows. If there are no arrows, press the seam allowances however you wish.

1. Layer each 3¾"-wide floral strip with a 3¾"-wide bright blue strip, right sides together, to make five contrasting strip pairs. From the strip pairs, cut 48 squares, 3¾" x 3¾". Cut the layered squares in half diagonally. Do not separate the triangle pairs.

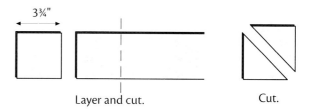

Layer and cut. Cut.

2. Chain stitch the triangle pairs along the long edges to make 96 half-square-triangle units.

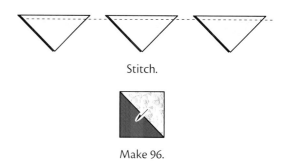

Stitch.

Make 96.

3. Cut the half-square-triangle units in half diagonally as shown. Join the resulting pieces to make 96 quarter-square-triangle units. Note that two divided half-square-triangle units will make two quarter-square-triangle units, but you must "mix and match" the pieces from both units as shown.

Cut. Mix and match. Make 96.

4. Join the units from step 3 and the 3" floral and green squares to make 48 unit A.

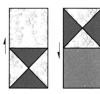

Unit A.
Make 48.

5. Join 24 of the 1¾" x 5½" floral rectangles and the 1¾" pink squares to make 12 unit B.

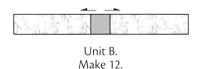

Unit B.
Make 12.

6. Join units A and B and the remaining floral rectangles to make 12 Chickadee Quadrille blocks.

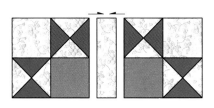

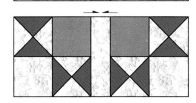

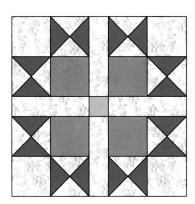

Make 12.

ASSEMBLING AND FINISHING THE QUILT

Basic instructions for borders, backing, and binding begin on page 14.

1. Set the blocks, setting squares, and setting triangles together in diagonal rows as shown. Press the seam allowances toward the setting pieces. Add the corner setting triangles last.

2. Trim and square up the edges of the quilt, leaving 1¼" outside the block points to allow for float.
3. Add the inner border using the 1"-wide pink strips.
4. Add the middle border using the 2½"-wide green strips.
5. Add the outer border using the 3½"-wide bright blue strips.
6. Seam the backing fabric. The seam will run lengthwise of the quilt.
7. Layer the quilt top with batting and backing; baste.
8. Hand or machine quilt.
9. Bind the quilt with the bright blue strips.

CHURN DASH

Pieced by Tina Tomsen and Kris Huber

Finished block: 7½" x 7½"
Finished quilt: 53" x 63⅝"

MATERIALS

Yardage is based on 42"-wide fabric.

¾ yard of pink print for blocks, setting pieces, and binding

½ yard *each* of 4 additional pink prints for blocks, setting pieces, and binding

4 strips, exactly 3⅞" wide x about 21" long, of additional pink prints for blocks (different from those above)

1 yard of medium blue print for blocks, setting pieces, and binding

1 fat quarter (18" x 20") of medium green print for setting pieces

1 rectangle, 9" x about 21", of medium green plaid for blocks

5 rectangles, 7" x about 21", of assorted white prints for blocks

5 rectangles, 11" x about 21", of assorted dark blue prints for blocks

3⅝ yards of fabric for backing

59" x 70" piece of batting

CUTTING

*All cutting dimensions include ¼"-wide seam allowances. **Note:** You may want to wait until after your blocks are pieced before cutting setting squares and triangles, in case your blocks measure larger or smaller than the expected 8" x 8" (raw edge to raw edge).*

From the ¾ yard of pink print, cut:

1 strip, 8" x 42"; crosscut into 4 setting squares, 8" x 8"

1 strip, 2" x 42". Cut the strip in half widthwise to make 2 strips, 2" x about 21".

2 squares, 11½" x 11½"; cut the squares in half diagonally to make 4 corner setting triangles

From *each* of any 3 of the 4 additional pink prints, cut:

1 square, 11⅞" x 11⅞" (3 total); cut the squares into quarters diagonally to make 12 side setting triangles (you'll use 10)

From the remainder of *each* of the 4 additional pink prints, cut:

3 setting squares, 8" x 8" (12 total)

1 strip, 2" x 42" (4 total); cut the strip in half widthwise to make 8 strips, 2" x about 21"

From the medium green plaid, cut:

1 strip, 3⅞" x about 21"

2 strips, 2" x about 21"

From *each* of the 5 assorted white prints, cut:

1 strip, 3⅞" x about 21" (5 total)

1 strip, 2" x about 21" (5 total)

From *each* of the 5 assorted dark blue prints, cut:

2 strips, 3⅞" x about 21" (10 total)

5 squares, 2" x 2" (25 total)

From the medium blue print, cut:

1 strip, 8" x 42"; crosscut into 4 setting squares, 8" x 8"

1 square, 11⅞" x 11⅞"; cut into quarters diagonally to make 4 side setting triangles

1 strip, 2" x about 21"

From the medium green print, cut:

4 setting squares, 8" x 8"

From the remaining pieces of pink and medium blue prints, cut:

Enough strips to make approximately 255" of binding when pieced together

MAKING THE BLOCKS

Press the seam allowances in the direction of the arrows. If there are no arrows, press the seam allowances however you wish.

1. Join each 2" x 21" white, green plaid, and blue strip to a 2" x 21" pink strip to make 10 strip units. From these strip units, cut 100 segments, 2" wide.

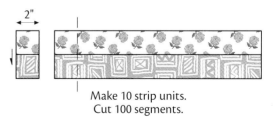

Make 10 strip units.
Cut 100 segments.

2. Layer each 3⅞"-wide white, green plaid, and pink strip with a 3⅞"-wide dark blue strip, right sides together, to make 10 contrasting strip pairs. From these strip pairs, cut 50 squares, 3⅞" x 3⅞". Cut the layered squares in half diagonally. Do not separate the triangle pairs.

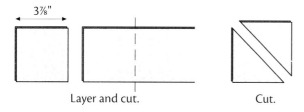

Layer and cut.   Cut.

3. Chain stitch the triangle pairs along the long edges to make 100 half-square-triangle units.

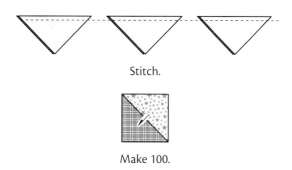

Stitch.

Make 100.

4. Randomly join the segments from step 1, the units from step 3, and the dark blue 2" squares to make 25 Churn Dash blocks.

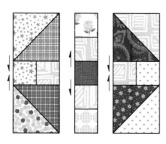

Make 25.

ASSEMBLING AND FINISHING THE QUILT

Basic instructions for borders, backing, and binding begin on page 14.

1. Set the blocks, the 8" setting squares, and the setting triangles together in diagonal rows as shown. Press the seam allowances toward the setting pieces.

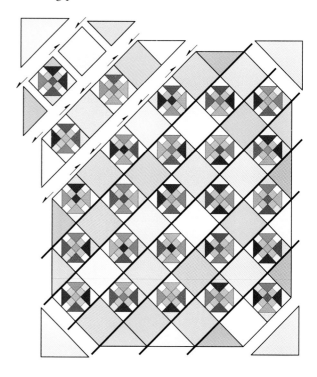

2. Seam the backing fabric. The seam will run crosswise of the quilt.
3. Layer the quilt top with batting and backing; baste.
4. Hand or machine quilt.
5. Bind the quilt with the assorted pink and medium blue strips.

COUNTERCHANGE CROSS

Pieced and quilted by Julie Wilkinson Kimberlin

Finished block: 9" x 9"
Finished quilt: 57" x 66"

MATERIALS

Yardage is based on 42"-wide fabric.

1⅞ yards of turquoise print for outer border and binding

1⅝ yards of light print for blocks

9 strips, exactly 3½" wide x about 42" long, of assorted turquoise and/or purple prints for blocks

9 strips, exactly 2" wide x about 42" long, of *different* turquoise and/or purple prints for blocks

⅜ yard of deep purple striped fabric for inner border

4 yards of fabric for backing

63" x 72" piece of batting

CUTTING

All cutting dimensions include ¼"-wide seam allowances.

From the light print, cut:
9 strips, 3½" x 42"
9 strips, 2" x 42"

From the deep purple striped fabric, cut:
7 border strips, 1¼" x 42"

From the turquoise print for outer border and binding, cut:
7 border strips, 5¾" x 42"
7 binding strips

MAKING THE BLOCKS

To avoid having to twist seam allowances on the back to make the seams butt together properly, you'll press all the seam allowances open.

1. Join the 3½"-wide light strips, the 3½"-wide turquoise and/or purple strips, the 2"-wide light strips, and the 2"-wide turquoise and/or purple strips to make nine strip units. Combine the turquoise and/or purple strips at random. From *each* strip unit, cut seven segments 3½" wide (63 total) and seven segments 2" wide (63 total). You'll use 60 segments of each width and have three of each width left over.

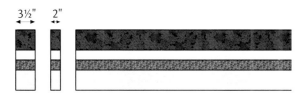

Make 9 strip units.
Cut 7 segments, 3½" wide, and
7 segments, 2" wide, from each.

2. Randomly join the 3½"-wide segments and the 2"-wide segments to make 60 units as shown.

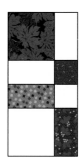

Make 60.

3. Randomly join the units from step 2 to make 30 Counterchange Cross blocks.

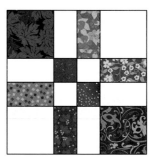

Make 30.

ASSEMBLING AND FINISHING THE QUILT

Basic instructions for borders, backing, and binding begin on page 14.

1. Set the blocks together as shown in the photo on page 45. Note that the blocks are oriented with the turquoise and/or purple corners at the upper left and lower right. Press the seam allowances open or in opposite directions from row to row.

2. Add the inner border using the 1¼"-wide deep purple striped strips.

3. Add the outer border using the 5¾"-wide turquoise strips.

4. Seam the backing fabric. The seam will run crosswise of the quilt.

5. Layer the quilt top with batting and backing; baste.

6. Hand or machine quilt.

7. Bind the quilt with the turquoise strips.

CRAB POT

Pieced and quilted by Rhoda Walker

Finished block: 10" x 10"
Finished quilt: 80" x 100"

MATERIALS

Yardage is based on 42"-wide fabric.

2⅓ yards of red-violet print for border and binding

½ yard *each* of 11 assorted red-violet prints for blocks

½ yard *each* of 11 assorted blue-violet prints for blocks

7⅞ yards of fabric for backing

86" x 106" piece of batting

CUTTING

All cutting dimensions include ¼"-wide seam allowances.

From *each* of the 11 assorted red-violet prints, cut:

1 strip, 4½" x 42" (11 total); crosscut *each* strip into:
  3 squares, 4½" x 4½" (33 total)
  6 rectangles, 1½" x 4½" (66 total)

3 strips, 2½" x 42" (33 total); crosscut *2 strips* of each print into 6 rectangles, 2½" x 10½" (66 total). Crosscut *each* of the remaining strips into 6 rectangles, 2½" x 6½" (66 total).

1 strip, 1½" x 42" (11 total); crosscut *each* strip into 6 rectangles, 1½" x 6½" (66 total)

From *each* of the 11 assorted blue-violet prints, cut:

1 strip, 4½" x 42" (11 total); crosscut *each* strip into:
  3 squares, 4½" x 4½" (33 total)
  6 rectangles, 1½" x 4½" (66 total)

3 strips, 2½" x 42" (33 total); crosscut *2 strips* of each print into 6 rectangles, 2½" x 10½" (66 total). Crosscut *each* of the remaining strips into 6 rectangles, 2½" x 6½" (66 total).

1 strip, 1½" x 42" (11 total); crosscut *each* strip into 6 rectangles, 1½" x 6½" (66 total)

From the red-violet print for border and binding, cut:

9 border strips, 5½" x 42"

10 binding strips

MAKING THE BLOCKS

Press the seam allowances in the direction of the arrows. **Note:** You'll be composing and making six blocks at a time using just two fabrics for each set of six blocks.

1. Using just one red-violet print and one blue-violet print, join 4½" squares and 1½" x 4½" rectangles to make three unit A and three unit B.

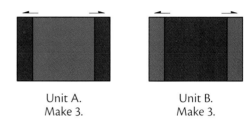

Unit A.
Make 3.

Unit B.
Make 3.

2. Join matching 1½" x 6½" rectangles to the units from step 1 to make three unit C and three unit D.

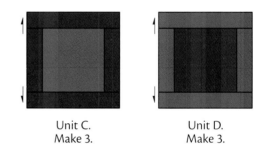

Unit C.
Make 3.

Unit D.
Make 3.

3. Join 2½" x 6½" rectangles to the units from step 2 to make three unit E and three unit F.

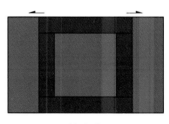

Unit E.
Make 3.

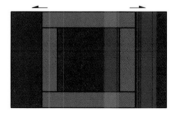

Unit F.
Make 3.

4. Join matching 2½" x 10½" rectangles to the units from step 3 to make three block A and three block B.

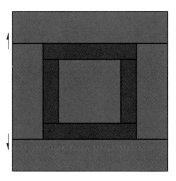

Block A.
Make 3.

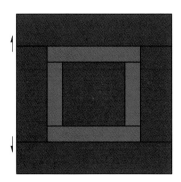

Block B.
Make 3.

5. Repeat steps 1–4 with the remaining squares and rectangles to make a total of 33 A blocks and 33 B blocks. Three of these blocks will be extras that you won't need for the quilt. Add borders to the blocks and use them to make throw pillows for your bed!

ASSEMBLING AND FINISHING THE QUILT

Basic instructions for borders, backing, and binding begin on page 14.

1. Set the blocks together as shown, alternating block A and block B and rotating the B blocks 90° so that the outside seams don't butt together.

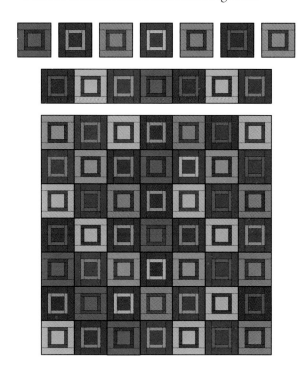

2. Add the border using the 5½"-wide red-violet strips.
3. Seam the backing fabric. You will have two seams that run crosswise of the quilt.
4. Layer the quilt top with batting and backing; baste.
5. Hand or machine quilt.
6. Bind the quilt with the red-violet strips.

CROW'S FOOT

Pieced and quilted by Judy Dafoe Hopkins

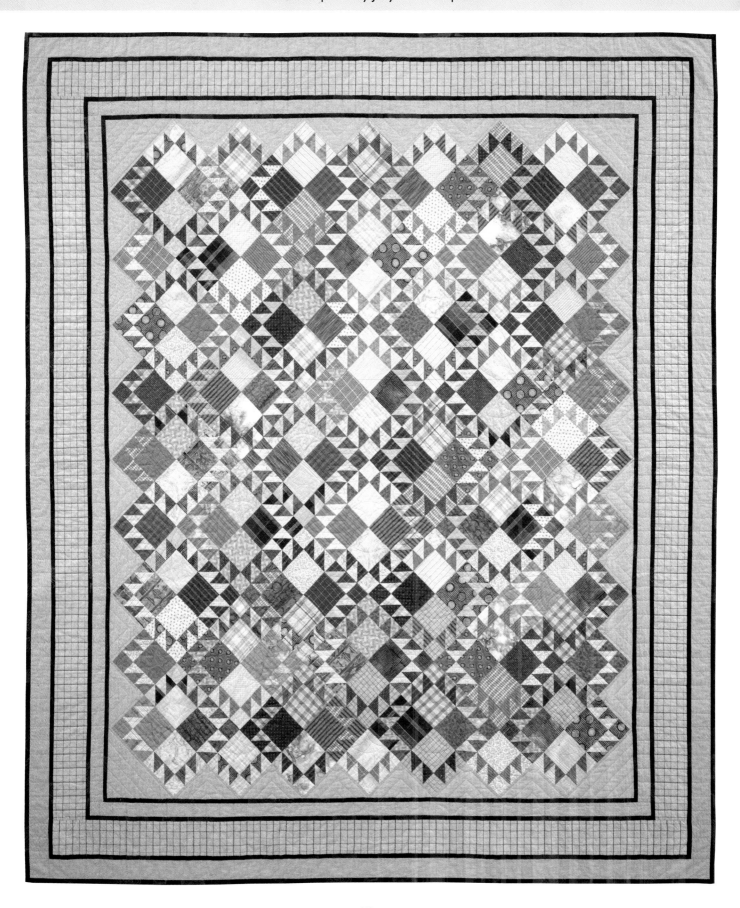

Finished block: 10½" x 10½"
Finished quilt: 77⅜" x 92¼"

MATERIALS

Yardage is based on 42"-wide fabric.

¼ yard *each* of 18 assorted light prints for blocks

¼ yard *each* of 18 assorted dark prints for blocks. Use blues, greens, and red-violets.

2⅛ yards of light blue checked fabric for setting triangles and borders

1½ yards of red-violet print for borders and binding

1⅛ yards of light blue windowpane-checked fabric for border

7 yards of fabric for backing

84" x 99" piece of batting

CUTTING

All cutting dimensions include ¼"-wide seam allowances.

From *each* of the 18 assorted light prints, cut:

1 strip, 2⅝" x 42" (18 total); crosscut *each* strip into 8 rectangles, 2⅝" x 5¼" (144 total)*

4 squares, 4" x 4" (72 total)

4 squares, 2¼" x 2¼" (72 total)

From *each* of the 18 assorted dark prints, cut:

1 strip, 2⅝" x 42" (18 total); crosscut *each* strip into 8 rectangles, 2⅝" x 5¼" (144 total)*

4 squares, 4" x 4" (72 total)

4 squares, 2¼" x 2¼" (72 total)

From the light blue checked fabric, cut:

2 strips, 9⅜" x 42"; crosscut into 7 squares, 9⅜" x 9⅜". Cut the squares into quarters diagonally to make 28 side setting triangles.

2 squares, 9" x 9"; cut the squares in half diagonally to make 4 corner setting triangles

8 border strips, 2" x 42"

9 border strips, 2¾" x 42"

From the red-violet print, cut:

25 border strips, 1" x 42"

9 binding strips

From the light blue windowpane-checked fabric, cut:

8 border strips, 4¼" x 42"

*If your fabric is less than 42" wide, cut the eighth rectangle from scraps after cutting the squares.

MAKING THE BLOCKS

Press the seam allowances in the direction of the arrows. To avoid having to twist seam allowances on the back to make the seams butt together properly, you'll press some of the seam allowances open (as indicated by double-headed arrows). If there are no arrows, press the seam allowances however you wish.

Note: You'll be composing and making one unit at a time using just two fabrics in each unit.

1. Compile 72 "dark sets" from the assorted dark print pieces, with each set containing one 2¼" dark square, one 4" dark square, and one dark rectangle, all from the same fabric.

   Repeat to compile 72 "light sets" from the assorted light print pieces.

2. Add one of the remaining light rectangles to each of the 72 dark sets. Add one of the remaining dark rectangles to each of the 72 light sets.

3. *Work with one set at a time, starting with the dark sets.* Layer the light and dark rectangles, right sides together, to make a contrasting rectangle pair. From the layered pair, cut two squares, 2⅝" x 2⅝". Cut the layered squares in half diagonally. Do not separate the triangle pairs.

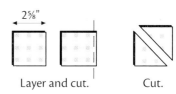

Layer and cut.   Cut.

4. Chain stitch the triangle pairs along the long edges to make four half-square-triangle units.

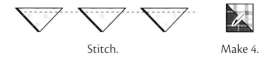

Stitch.   Make 4.

5. Join the units from step 4 and the matching 2¼" and 4" dark squares to make one unit A.

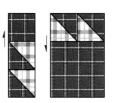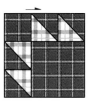

Unit A

6. Repeat steps 3–5 with the remaining dark sets to make a total of 72 unit A.

7. Repeat steps 3–5 with the light sets to make 72 unit B (you'll use 70).

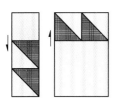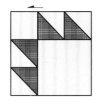

Unit B.
Make 72.

8. Randomly join 64 unit A and 64 unit B to make 32 Crow's Foot blocks using two A units and two B units in each block.

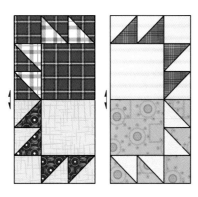

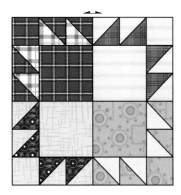

Make 32.

9. Join the 9⅜" blue checked side setting triangles to the remaining A and B units to make eight dark and six light pieced setting triangles.

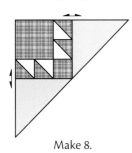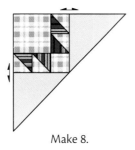

Make 8.   Make 8.

ASSEMBLING AND FINISHING THE QUILT

Basic instructions for borders, backing, and binding begin on page 14.

1. Randomly join the blocks and the pieced setting triangles in diagonal rows, as shown. Note that the blocks are oriented with the large light squares falling on the vertical; the dark setting triangles are used on the sides, and the light setting triangles appear on the top and bottom. Press the seam allowances in opposite directions from row to row. Add the corner setting triangles last.

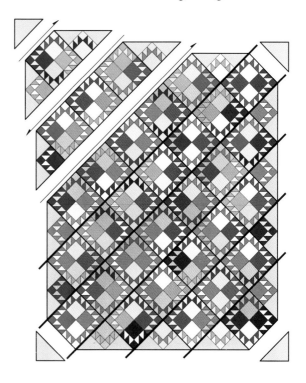

2. Trim and square up the edges of the quilt, leaving at least ¼" outside the block points.

3. Add borders in the following order: 1"-wide red-violet strips, 2"-wide blue checked strips, 1"-wide red-violet strips, 4¼"-wide blue windowpane-checked strips, 1"-wide red-violet strips, and 2¾"-wide blue checked strips.

4. Seam the backing fabric. You'll have two seams that run crosswise of the quilt.

5. Layer the quilt top with batting and backing; baste.

6. Hand or machine quilt.

7. Bind the quilt with the red-violet strips.

CUTTING CORNERS

Pieced and quilted by Elise Rose

Finished block: 7½" x 7½"
Finished quilt: 54½" x 69½"

MATERIALS

Yardage is based on 42"-wide fabric.

8 fat quarters (18" x 20") of assorted white-on-white prints for blocks and binding

8 fat quarters of assorted indigo prints for blocks

1⅓ yards of white-on-white print for outer border and binding

¼ yard of indigo print for inner border*

3¾ yards of fabric for backing

61" x 76" piece of batting

Use one of the fabrics you used for the blocks or a completely different fabric.

CUTTING

All cutting dimensions include ¼"-wide seam allowances.

From *each* of the 8 white-on-white fat quarters, cut:

3 strips, 4¼" x 18" (24 total); crosscut into 96 squares, 4¼" x 4¼"

2 strips, 2⅜" x 18" (16 total); crosscut into 96 squares, 2⅜" x 2⅜"

1 binding strip (8 total)

From *each* of the 8 indigo fat quarters, cut:

3 strips, 4¼" x 18" (24 total); crosscut into 96 squares, 4¼" x 4¼"

2 strips, 2⅜" x 18" (16 total); crosscut into 96 squares, 2⅜" x 2⅜"

From the indigo print for inner border, cut:

6 strips, 1¼" x 42"

From the white-on-white print for outer border and binding, cut:

7 border strips, 4½" x 42"

4 binding strips

MAKING THE BLOCKS

Press the seam allowances in the direction of the arrows. To avoid having to twist seam allowances on the back to make the seams butt together properly, you'll press some of the seam allowances open (as indicated by double-headed arrows).

1. Align the 2⅜" indigo squares with the right-hand corners of the 4¼" white-on-white squares, right sides together. Draw a diagonal line from corner to corner on each of the indigo squares as shown and stitch on the lines. Trim to leave ¼"-wide seam allowances; press to make 96 unit A.

Stitch.　　Trim.　　Unit A.
Make 96.

2. Repeat step 1 with the 2⅜" white-on-white squares and the 4¼" indigo squares to make 96 unit B.

Unit B.
Make 96.

SAVE THE CORNERS

Seam the cut-off corners and use the resulting half-square-triangle units as part of a sawtooth border or for another project.

3. Randomly join the units from steps 1 and 2 to make 48 Cutting Corners blocks, using two A units and two B units in each block.

Make 48.

ASSEMBLING AND FINISHING THE QUILT

Basic instructions for borders, backing, and binding begin on page 14.

1. Set the blocks together as shown. Note that the blocks should be oriented so the white-on-white corners are at the upper left and lower right. Press the seam allowances in opposite directions from row to row.

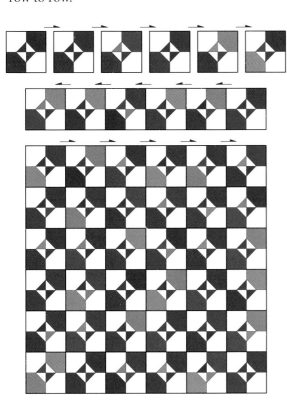

2. Add the inner border using the 1¼"-wide indigo strips.

3. Add the outer border using the 4½"-wide white-on-white strips.

4. Seam the backing fabric. The seam will run crosswise of the quilt.
5. Layer the quilt top with batting and backing; baste.
6. Hand or machine quilt.
7. Bind the quilt with the assorted white-on-white strips.

DANDELION WINE

Pieced by Judy Dafoe Hopkins; quilted by Becky Crook

Finished block: 4½" x 4½"
Finished quilt: 57" x 85½"

MATERIALS

Yardage is based on 42"-wide fabric.

2⅞ yards of dandelion print (or other interesting print) for wide vertical bars

1¼ yards of tan print for blocks and binding

⅝ yard of dark tan print for blocks

10 strips, exactly 2¾" wide x at least 24" long, of assorted light prints for blocks

10 strips, exactly 2¾" wide x at least 24" long, of assorted dark prints for blocks. Use greens, blues, and reds.

½ yard of dark brown print for narrow vertical bars

5¾ yards of fabric for backing

63" x 91" piece of batting

CUTTING

All cutting dimensions include ¼"-wide seam allowances.

From the tan print, cut:
6 strips, 2¾" x 42"
8 binding strips

From the dark tan print, cut:
6 strips, 2¾" x 42"

From the dark brown print, cut:
9 strips, 1½" x 42"

From the *lengthwise grain* of the dandelion print, cut:
5 strips, 7½" x at least 88"

MAKING THE BLOCKS

Press the seam allowances in the direction of the arrows. If there are no arrows, press the seam allowances however you wish.

1. Join each 2¾"-wide tan strip to a 2¾"-wide dark tan strip to make six strip units. From these strip units, cut 72 segments, 2¾" wide.

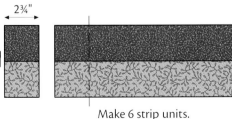

Make 6 strip units.
Cut 72 segments.

2. Join the segments from step 1 to make 36 unit A.

Unit A.
Make 36.

3. Randomly join each 2¾"-wide light strip to a 2¾"-wide dark strip to make 10 strip units. From *each* strip unit, cut eight segments, 2¾" wide (80 total).

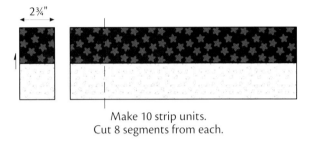

Make 10 strip units.
Cut 8 segments from each.

4. Join identical segments from step 3 to make 40 unit B.

Unit B.
Make 40.

ASSEMBLING AND FINISHING THE QUILT

Basic instructions for borders, backing, and binding begin on page 14.

1. Join the 1½"-wide dark brown strips end to end to make one continuous strip. Cut this strip into four equal pieces, each at least 88" long.

2. Join units A and B, the 1½"-wide dark brown strips, and the 7½"-wide dandelion print strips as shown in the photo on the facing page, trimming the dark brown and dandelion print strips to fit the block rows. Note that the A and B units are oriented with the lighter squares running diagonally from lower left to upper right.

3. Seam the backing fabric. The seam will run lengthwise of the quilt.

4. Layer the quilt top with batting and backing; baste.

5. Hand or machine quilt.

6. Bind the quilt with the tan strips.

DOMINO AND SQUARE

Pieced and quilted by Anita Daggett

Finished block: 15" x 15"
Finished quilt: 61" x 78"

MATERIALS

Yardage is based on 42"-wide fabric.

3⅞ yards of off-white fabric for block backgrounds, sashing, border, and binding
12 strips, 4¾" x 26", of assorted red prints for blocks
12 strips, 2⅝" x 22", of assorted tan prints for blocks
12 strips, 2⅝" x 21", of assorted light prints for blocks
12 strips, 2⅝" x 12", of assorted black prints for blocks
5¼ yards of fabric for backing
67" x 84" piece of batting

CUTTING

All cutting dimensions include ¼"-wide seam allowances. ***Note:*** *You may want to wait until your blocks are pieced before cutting sashing pieces and strips, in case your blocks measure larger or smaller than the expected 15½" x 15½" (raw edge to raw edge).*

From *each* of the 12 assorted black strips, cut:
4 squares, 2⅝" x 2⅝" (48 total)

From *each* of the 12 assorted tan strips, cut:
8 squares, 2⅝" x 2⅝" (96 total)

From the off-white fabric, cut:
4 strips, 4¼" x 42"; crosscut into 36 squares, 4¼" x 4¼". Cut the squares into quarters diagonally to make 144 triangles. Pin a note that says "4¼" to these triangles.
3 strips, 3⅞" x 42"; crosscut into 24 squares, 3⅞" x 3⅞". Cut the squares in half diagonally to make 48 triangles. Pin a note that says "3⅞" to these triangles.
4 sashing strips, 2½" x 42"
1 strip, 15½" x 42"; crosscut into 8 sashing pieces, 2½" x 15½"

From the *lengthwise grain* of the remaining off-white fabric, cut:
4 border strips, 6½" x at least 69"
5 binding strips

From *one end* of *each* of the 12 assorted red strips, cut:
1 square, 4¾" x 4¾" (12 total)

MAKING THE BLOCKS

For ease of construction, press the seam allowances open.

1. Sort the 2⅝" black and tan squares into 12 piles, with each pile containing four matching black squares and eight matching tan squares.
2. *Work with one pile at a time.* Join four matching black squares, eight matching tan squares, and twelve 4¼" off-white triangles to make four unit A.

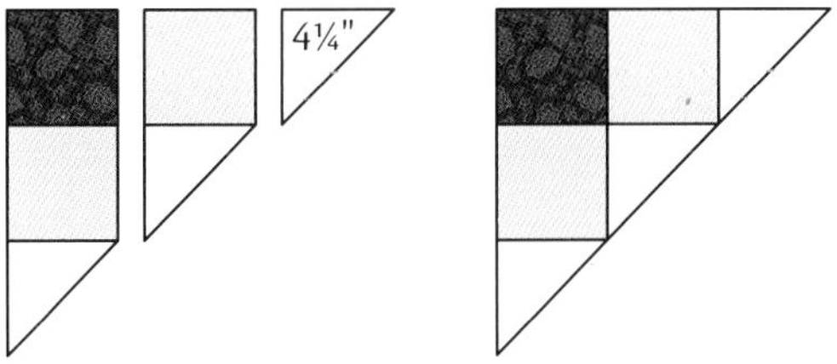

Unit A.
Make 4.

3. Repeat step 2 with the remaining 11 piles. When you've finished stitching all 12 piles, you'll have 12 sets of unit A, each set containing four identical units.
4. Join each 2⅝"-wide light strip to the remainder of a 4¾"-wide red strip to make 12 strip units. From each strip unit, cut four segments, 4¾" wide (48 total).

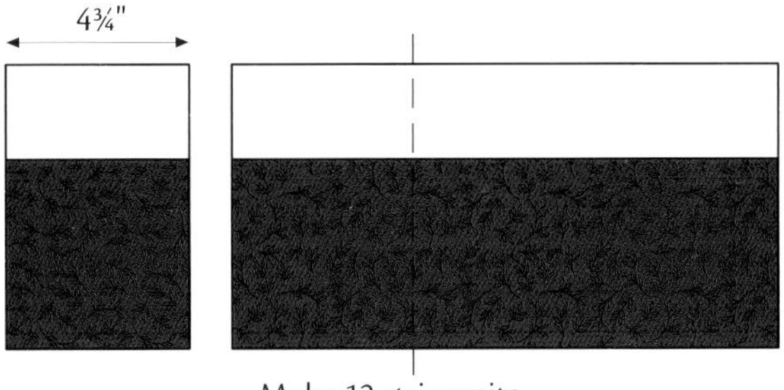

Make 12 strip units.
Cut 4 segments from each.

5. Join 24 segments from step 4 and the loose 4¾" red squares to make 12 unit B. Use matching red squares in each unit.

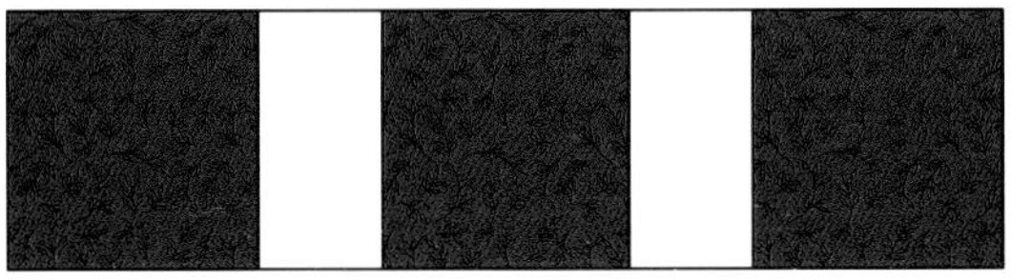

Unit B.
Make 12.

6. Join units A and B and the remaining segments from step 4 to make 12 unit C, with each unit containing one red print, one black print, and one tan print.

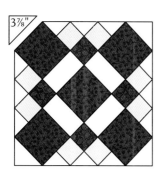

Unit C.
Make 12.

7. Join 3⅞" off-white triangles to the corners of the C units to make 12 Domino and Square blocks.

Make 12.

ASSEMBLING AND FINISHING THE QUILT

Basic instructions for borders, backing, and binding begin on page 14.

1. Set the blocks together in four rows, with each row containing three blocks and two 2½" x 15½" off-white sashing pieces as shown. Press the seam allowances toward the sashing pieces.

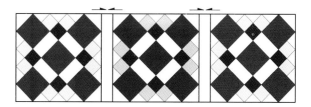

2. Join the 2½"-wide off-white sashing strips end to end, press the seam allowances open, and cut three sashing strips to the length of the block-and-sashing rows you made in step 1. Set the block rows and the sashing strips together as shown. Press the seam allowances toward the sashing strips.

3. Add the border using the 6½"-wide off-white strips.
4. Seam the backing fabric. The seam will run lengthwise of the quilt.
5. Layer the quilt top with batting and backing; baste.
6. Hand or machine quilt.
7. Bind the quilt with the off-white strips.

DOUBLE FOUR-PATCH

Pieced by Michelle A. Hall; quilted by Janet Fogg

Finished block: 6" x 6"
Finished quilt: 60" x 72"

MATERIALS

Yardage is based on 42"-wide fabric.

8 fat quarters (18" x 20") of assorted cream prints for blocks

8 fat quarters of assorted dark green and/or medium green prints for blocks

1½ yards of cream print for outer border*

1 yard of green print for inner border and binding*

4¼ yards of fabric for backing

66" x 78" piece of batting

Use one of the fabrics you used for the blocks or a completely different fabric.

CUTTING

All cutting dimensions include ¼"-wide seam allowances.

From *each* of the 8 assorted cream prints and 8 assorted green prints, cut:

4 strips, 2" x 21" (32 cream and 32 green strips total)

2 strips, 3½" x 21"; crosscut *each* strip into 5 squares, 3½" x 3½" (80 cream and 80 green squares total)

From the green print for inner border and binding, cut:

7 border strips, 1½" x 42"

8 binding strips

From the cream print for outer border, cut:

8 strips, 5½" x 42"

MAKING THE BLOCKS

Press the seam allowances in the direction of the arrows. If there are no arrows, press the seam allowances however you wish.

1. Randomly join each 2"-wide cream strip to a 2"-wide green strip to make 32 strip units. From each strip unit, cut 10 segments, 2" wide (320 total).

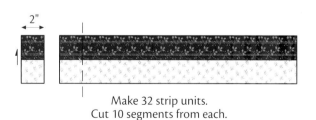

Make 32 strip units.
Cut 10 segments from each.

2. Randomly join the segments from step 1 to make 160 four-patch units.

Make 160.

3. Randomly join the four-patch units from step 2 and the 3½" green and cream squares to make 80 unit A and 80 unit B *exactly* as shown. Note that the small light squares always run from lower left to upper right.

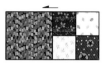

Unit A.
Make 80.

Unit B.
Make 80.

4. Randomly join the units from step 3 to make 40 block A and 40 block B.

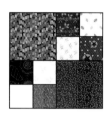
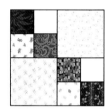

Block A.
Make 40.

Block B.
Make 40.

ASSEMBLING AND FINISHING THE QUILT

Basic instructions for borders, backing, and binding begin on page 14.

1. Set the blocks together as shown in the photo on page 61. Note that all the blocks are oriented so the small light squares run diagonally from lower left to upper right.

2. Add the inner border using the 1½"-wide green strips.

3. Add the outer border using the 5½"-wide cream strips.

4. Seam the backing fabric. The seam will run crosswise of the quilt.

5. Layer the quilt top with batting and backing; baste.

6. Hand or machine quilt.

7. Bind the quilt with the green strips.

EQUINOX

Pieced by Judy Dafoe Hopkins; quilted by Carol Parks

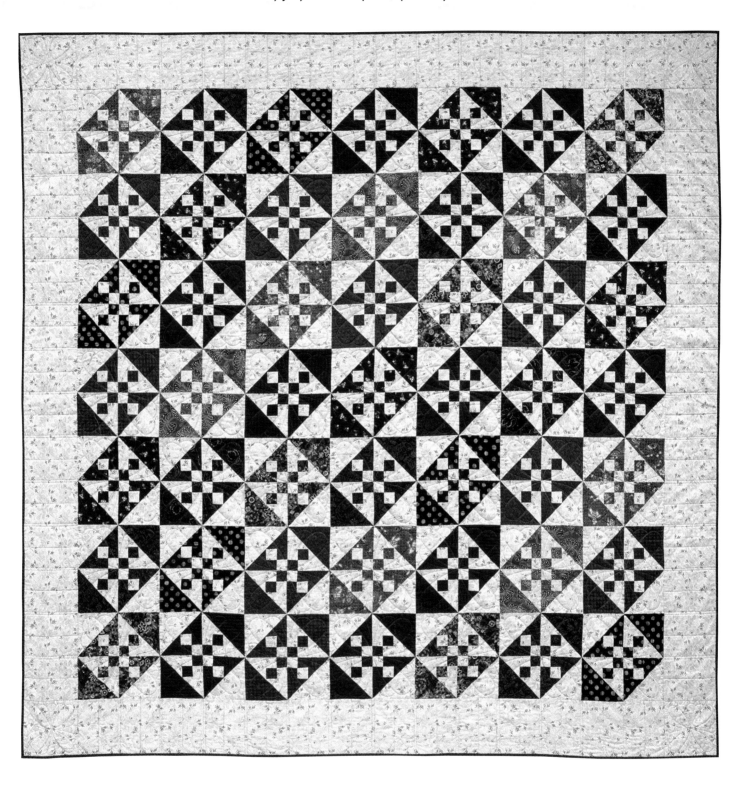

Finished block: 12" x 12"
Finished quilt: 100" x 100"

MATERIALS

Yardage is based on 42"-wide fabric.

7⅞ yards of light print for blocks and border

25 rectangles, 16" x 18", of assorted indigo prints for blocks*

⅞ yard of indigo striped fabric for binding

9¾ yards of fabric for backing

106" x 106" piece of batting

Use the same fabric more than once, if you wish.

CUTTING

All cutting dimensions include ¼"-wide seam allowances.

From the light print, cut:

2 strips, 18" x 42"; crosscut the strips into 40 rectangles, 2" x 18"

5 strips, 2" x 42"; crosscut the strips into 10 rectangles, 2" x 18". Add these to the rectangles you cut above, for a total of 50 rectangles.

10 strips, 6⅞" x 42"; crosscut the strips into 50 squares, 6⅞" x 6⅞". Cut the squares in half diagonally to make 100 triangles.

10 strips, 3⅞" x 42"; crosscut the strips into 100 squares, 3⅞" x 3⅞". Cut the squares in half diagonally to make 200 triangles.

From the *lengthwise grain* of the remaining light print, cut:

4 border strips, 8½" x at least 102"

From *each* of the 25 assorted indigo prints, cut:

2 strips, 2" x 18" (50 total)

1 strip, 6⅞" x 18" (25 total); crosscut each strip into 2 squares, 6⅞" x 6⅞" (50 total). Cut the squares in half diagonally to make 100 triangles.

1 strip, 3⅞" x 18" (25 total); crosscut each strip into 4 squares, 3⅞" x 3⅞" (100 total). Cut the squares in half diagonally to make 200 triangles.

From the indigo striped fabric, cut:

11 binding strips

USING LEFTOVER FABRIC

Use the leftovers from the light print to trim pillowcases, make throw pillows or pillow shams, or as part of a pieced backing.

MAKING THE BLOCKS

Press the seam allowances in the direction of the arrows.

1. Join each 2" x 18" light rectangle to a 2" x 18" indigo rectangle to make 50 strip units. From *each* strip unit, cut eight segments, 2" wide (400 total).

2"

Make 50 strip units.
Cut 8 segments from each.

2. Join the step 1 segments to make 200 four-patch units, matching the indigo prints in each unit.

Make 200.

3. Join the 3⅞" light and indigo triangles to the units from step 2 to make 100 unit A and 100 unit B *exactly* as shown, matching the indigo prints in each unit B. Pay particular attention to the orientation of the indigo squares.

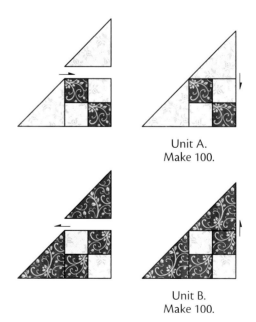

Unit A.
Make 100.

Unit B.
Make 100.

4. Join the 6⅞" indigo and light triangles to the units from step 3 to make 100 unit C and 100 unit D, matching the indigo prints in each C unit.

Unit C.
Make 100.

Unit D.
Make 100.

5. Join the units to make 50 Equinox blocks, matching the indigo prints in each block. One of these blocks will be an extra that you won't need for the quilt. Add borders to it and make a throw pillow for your bed!

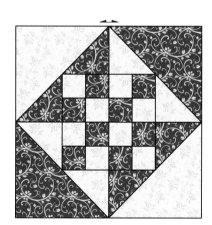

Make 50.

ALTERNATE SETTING CHOICES

Because the C and D units are divided diagonally into light and dark sections, you could arrange them in any Log Cabin setting, such as Barn Raising or Straight Furrows, instead of joining them to make Equinox blocks.

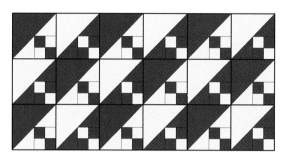

Straight Furrows

ASSEMBLING AND FINISHING THE QUILT

Basic instructions for borders, backing, and binding begin on page 14.

1. Set the blocks together as shown in the photo on page 63. Note that the blocks are oriented with the large light print triangles at the upper left and lower right. Press the seam allowances in opposite directions from row to row.
2. Add the border using the 8½"-wide light print strips.
3. Seam the backing fabric. You will have two seams that run crosswise of the quilt.
4. Layer the quilt top with batting and backing; baste.
5. Hand or machine quilt.
6. Bind the quilt with the indigo striped strips.

Flying Geese

Pieced by Judy Dafoe Hopkins; quilted by Carol Parks

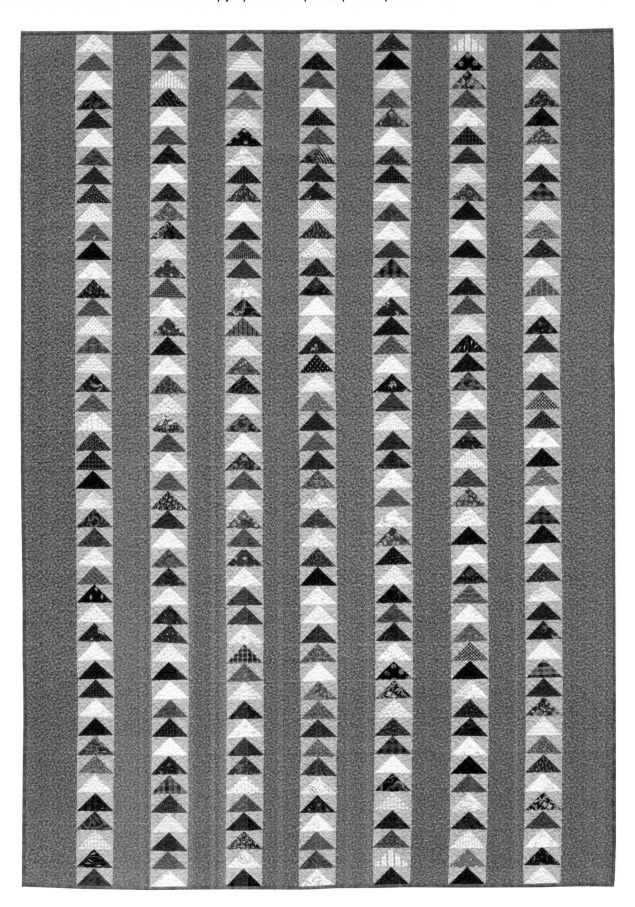

Finished block: 2" x 4"
Finished quilt: 63½" x 90"

MATERIALS

Yardage is based on 42"-wide fabric.

3⅛ yards of cheddar print for block backgrounds

2⅞ yards of dark pink print for setting strips

25 strips, exactly 2½" wide x about 42" long, of assorted dark prints for blocks. Use blues, greens, blacks, and browns.*

15 strips, exactly 2½" wide x about 42" long, of assorted light prints for blocks*

¾ yard of dark pink print for binding**

5⅞ yards of fabric for backing

70" x 96" piece of batting

Use the same fabric more than once, if you wish.

**Use the same fabric you used for the setting strips, if you wish.*

CUTTING

All cutting dimensions include ¼"-wide seam allowances.

From *each* of the 25 assorted dark strips and 15 assorted light strips, cut:

8 rectangles, 2½" x 4½" (320 total; you'll use 315)

From the cheddar print, cut:

40 strips, 2½" x 42"; crosscut the strips into 630 squares, 2½" x 2½"

From the *lengthwise grain* of the dark pink print for setting strips, cut:

2 strips, 6¼" wide x at least 92" long

6 strips, 4½" wide x at least 92" long

From the dark pink print for binding, cut:

9 strips

MAKING THE UNITS

Press the seam allowances in the direction of the arrows.

1. Align 2½" cheddar squares with the left-hand corners of the 2½" x 4½" assorted light and dark rectangles, right sides together. Draw a diagonal line from corner to corner on each of the cheddar squares as shown and stitch on the lines. Trim to leave ¼" seam allowances; press.

Stitch.

Trim.

Make 315.

2. Align the remaining 2½" cheddar squares with the right-hand corners of the units from step 1, right sides together. Draw, stitch, trim, and press as before.

Stitch.

Trim.

Make 315.

SAVE THE CORNERS

Seam the cut-off corners and use the resulting half-square-triangle units as part of a sawtooth border or for another project.

ASSEMBLING AND FINISHING THE QUILT

Basic instructions for borders, backing, and binding begin on page 14.

1. Randomly join the 315 flying-geese units to make seven strips, each containing 45 units, as shown in the photo on the facing page. Press the seam allowances however you wish.

2. Measure the length of the flying-geese strips and cut the 6¼"-wide and 4½"-wide dark pink setting strips to that measurement.

3. Join the flying-geese strips and the dark pink setting strips as shown in the photo. Note that the 6¼"-wide dark pink strips appear on the outside edges of the quilt. Press the seam allowances toward the setting strips.

4. Seam the backing fabric. The seam will run lengthwise of the quilt.

5. Layer the quilt top with batting and backing; baste.

6. Hand or machine quilt.

7. Bind the quilt with the dark pink strips.

GARDEN GAZEBO

Pieced and quilted by Dianna "Dee" Morrow

Finished block: 6" x 6"
Finished quilt: 65" x 82"

MATERIALS

Yardage is based on 42"-wide fabric.

3 gradations of peach fabrics:

1⅓ yards of light peach for blocks and setting pieces

1½ yards of medium peach for blocks and binding

1 yard of dark peach for blocks

4 gradations of gray fabrics:

⅝ yard of light gray for blocks

⅝ yard of light-medium gray for blocks

⅞ yard of medium gray for blocks and inner border

⅝ yard of dark-medium gray for blocks

1⅝ yards of medium-scale peach print for outer border

5½ yards of fabric for backing

71" x 88" piece of batting

CUTTING

All cutting dimensions include ¼"-wide seam allowances.

From the light peach fabric, cut:

1 strip, 9¾" x 42"; crosscut into 3 squares, 9¾" x 9¾".
   Cut the squares into quarters diagonally to make 12
   side setting triangles (you'll use 10).

1 strip, 6½" x 42"; crosscut into 6 squares, 6½" x 6½"

6 strips, 3½" x 42"; crosscut into 60 squares, 3½" x 3½"

2 squares, 5⅛" x 5⅛"; cut the squares in half diagonally
   to make 4 corner setting triangles

From the medium peach fabric, cut:

2 strips, 4¼" x 42"; crosscut into 12 squares, 4¼" x 4¼".
   Cut the squares into quarters diagonally to make
   48 triangles.

3 strips, 6⅞" x 42"; crosscut into 12 squares, 6⅞" x 6⅞"

8 binding strips

From the dark peach fabric, cut:

3 strips, 3⅞" x 42"; crosscut into 24 squares,
   3⅞" x 3⅞". Cut the squares in half diagonally to
   make 48 triangles.

3 strips, 6⅞" x 42"; crosscut into 12 squares, 6⅞" x 6⅞"

From *each* of the 4 gray fabrics, cut:

8 strips, 2" x 42" (32 total)

From the remaining medium gray fabric, cut:

8 border strips, 1½" x 42"

From the medium-scale peach print, cut:

8 border strips, 6½" x 42"

MAKING THE BLOCKS

Press the seam allowances in the direction of the arrows. To avoid having to twist seam allowances on the back to make the seams butt together properly, you'll press some of the seam allowances open (as indicated by double-headed arrows).

1. Join 4¼" medium peach triangles to 12 of the 3½" light peach squares to make 12 units (see "Stitching Tips for Square-in-a-Square Units" on page 12).

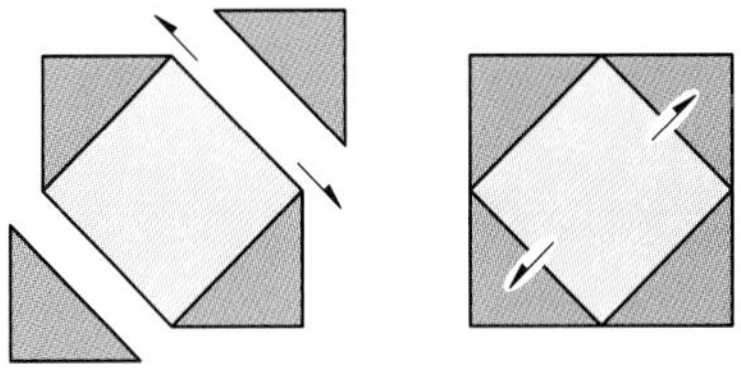

Make 12.

2. Join 3⅞" dark peach triangles to the units from step 1 to make 12 block A.

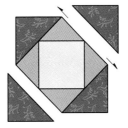 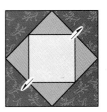

Block A.
Make 12.

3. Align a 3½" light peach square with the upper-left corner of each 6⅞" medium peach and dark peach square, right sides together. Draw a diagonal line from corner to corner on each light square and stitch on the line. Trim to leave ¼"-wide seam allowances; press.

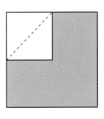 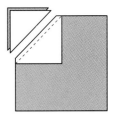

Stitch.　　　Trim.

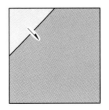 

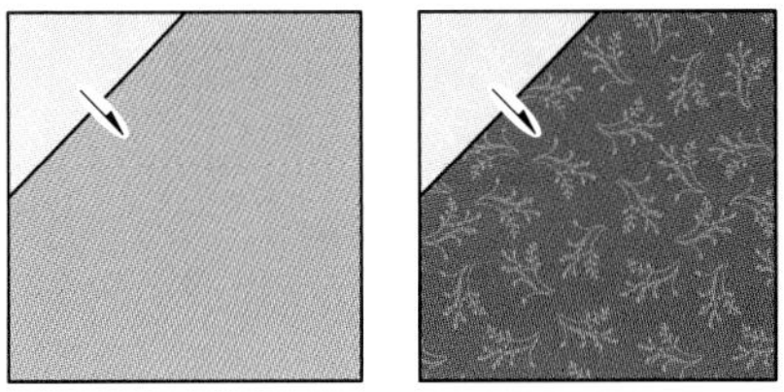

Press.

4. Align a 3½" light peach square with the lower-right corner of each unit from step 3, right sides together. Draw, stitch, trim, and press as before.

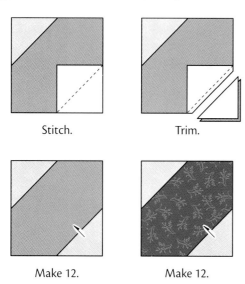

Stitch.　Trim.

Make 12.　Make 12.

SAVE THE CORNERS
Seam the cut-off corners and use the resulting half-square-triangle units as part of a sawtooth border or for another project.

5. Cut the units from step 4 in half diagonally as shown to make 48 triangle units.

Cut on the diagonal.

6. Join 34 of the triangle units to make 17 block B using one medium and one dark half in each block. The remaining triangle units will be used for the side setting pieces.

Block B.
Make 17.

7. Join the 2"-wide gray strips to make eight strip units, *exactly* as shown. From these strip units, cut 48 segments, 6½" wide, for block C.

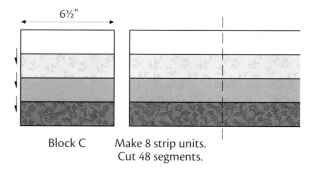

6½"

Block C　Make 8 strip units.
Cut 48 segments.

ASSEMBLING AND FINISHING THE QUILT
Basic instructions for borders, backing, and binding begin on page 14.

1. Set the blocks, the 6½" light peach squares, the 5⅛" and 9¾" light peach setting triangles, and the remaining triangle units from step 5 of "Making the Blocks" together in diagonal rows as shown. Press the seam allowances toward the C blocks.

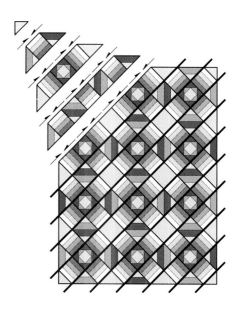

2. Add the inner border using the 1½"-wide medium gray strips.
3. Add the outer border using the 6½"-wide peach print strips.
4. Seam the backing fabric. The seam will run lengthwise of the quilt.
5. Layer the quilt top with batting and backing; baste.
6. Hand or machine quilt.
7. Bind the quilt with the medium peach strips.

GOLD NUGGETS

Pieced by Juli Thompson; quilted by Carol Parks

Finished block: 8½" x 8½"
Finished quilt: 61½" x 78½"

MATERIALS

Yardage is based on 42"-wide fabric.

⅓ yard *each* of 12 assorted yellow prints for blocks*

3 yards of multicolored focal print for blocks and outer border

1⅝ yards of purple print for blocks and binding

⅝ yard of lime green print for inner border

5¼ yards of fabric for backing

68" x 85" piece of batting

Use the same fabric more than once, if you wish.

CUTTING

All cutting dimensions include ¼"-wide seam allowances.

From the purple print, cut:
12 strips, 2½" x 42"
8 binding strips

From *each* of the 12 assorted yellow prints, cut:
1 strip, 2½" x 42" (12 total)
3 squares, 5⅛" x 5⅛" (36 total); cut the squares in half diagonally to make 72 triangles (you'll use 68)

From the multicolored focal print, cut:
6 strips, 5⅛" x 42"; crosscut into 36 squares, 5⅛" x 5⅛". Cut the squares in half diagonally to make 72 triangles.
8 border strips, 8" x 42"

From the lime green print, cut:
7 border strips, 2½" x 42"

USING LEFTOVER FABRIC

Use the leftovers to trim pillowcases, to make throw pillows or pillow shams, or as part of a pieced backing.

MAKING THE BLOCKS

Press the seam allowances in the direction of the arrows.

1. Randomly join the 2½"-wide yellow and purple strips to make four purple-yellow-purple strip units and four yellow-purple-yellow strip units as shown. Cut the number of 2½"-wide segments indicated.

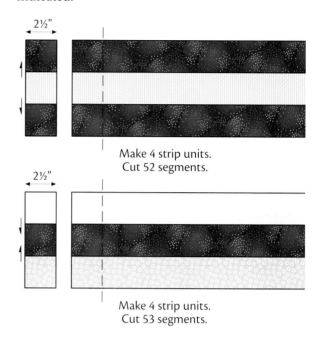

2½"

Make 4 strip units.
Cut 52 segments.

2½"

Make 4 strip units.
Cut 53 segments.

2. Randomly join the segments from step 1 to make 18 unit A and 17 unit B.

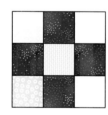

Unit A.
Make 18.

Unit B.
Make 17.

3. Join focal print triangles to the A units to make 18 block A (see "Stitching Tips for Square-in-a-Square Units" on page 12).

Block A.
Make 18.

4. Randomly join yellow triangles to the B units to make 17 block B.

Block B.
Make 17.

ASSEMBLING AND FINISHING THE QUILT

Basic instructions for borders, backing, and binding begin on page 14.

1. Set the blocks together as shown, alternating block A and block B. Press the seam allowances in opposite directions from row to row.

2. Add the inner border using the 2½"-wide lime green strips.
3. Add the outer border using the 8"-wide focal print strips.
4. Seam the backing fabric. The seam will run lengthwise of the quilt.
5. Layer the quilt top with batting and backing; baste.
6. Hand or machine quilt.
7. Bind the quilt with the purple strips.

GOLDEN SAMOVAR

Pieced and quilted by Elise Rose

Finished block: 10½" x 10½"
Finished quilt: 64¼" x 77"

MATERIALS

Yardage is based on 42"-wide fabric.

4¼ yards of lavender print for blocks, sashing pieces, outer border, and binding
1⅔ yards of white-on-white print for block backgrounds
1⅓ yards of coral print for blocks and inner border
1¼ yards of gold print for blocks and sashing squares
1 yard of maroon print for blocks
5⅛ yards of fabric for backing
71" x 83" piece of batting

CUTTING

All cutting dimensions include ¼"-wide seam allowances. ***Note:*** *You may want to wait until your blocks are pieced before cutting sashing pieces, in case your blocks measure larger or smaller than the expected 11" x 11" (raw edge to raw edge).*

From the white-on-white print, cut:
1 strip, 25" x 42"; crosscut into:
- 10 strips, 2⅝" x 25"
- 6 strips, 2¼" x 25"; crosscut into 60 squares, 2¼" x 2¼"

5 strips, 4¾" x 42"
2 strips, 2¼" x 42"; crosscut into 20 squares, 2¼" x 2¼". Add these to the 2¼" white squares you cut from the 25" strip, for a total of 80 squares.

From the coral print, cut:
1 strip, 25" x 42"; crosscut into:
- 4 strips, 2⅝" x 25"
- 1 strip, 2¼" x 25"; crosscut into 8 squares, 2¼" x 2¼"
- 2 squares, 4" x 4"

2 strips, 4¾" x 42"
8 border strips, 1" x 42"

From the maroon print, cut:
1 strip, 25" x 42"; crosscut into:
- 2 strips, 2⅝" x 25"
- 3 strips, 2¼" x 25"; crosscut into 24 squares, 2¼" x 2¼"
- 1 strip, 4" x 25"; crosscut into 6 squares, 4" x 4"

1 strip, 4¾" x 42"

From the gold print, cut:
1 strip, 25" x 42"; crosscut into:
- 2 strips, 2⅝" x 25"
- 3 strips, 2¼" x 25"; crosscut into 24 squares, 2¼" x 2¼"
- 1 strip, 4" x 25"; crosscut into 6 squares, 4" x 4"

1 strip, 4¾" x 42"
3 strips, 2¾" x 42"; crosscut into 30 sashing squares, 2¾" x 2¾"

From the lavender print, cut:
1 strip, 25" x 42"; crosscut into:
- 2 strips, 2⅝" x 25"
- 3 strips, 2¼" x 25"; crosscut into 24 squares, 2¼" x 2¼"
- 1 strip, 4" x 25"; crosscut into 6 squares, 4" x 4"

4 strips, 11" x 42"; crosscut into 49 sashing pieces, 2¾" x 11"
1 strip, 4¾" x 42"
8 border strips, 5½" x 42"
8 binding strips

MAKING THE BLOCKS

Press the seam allowances in the direction of the arrows. If there are no arrows, press the seam allowances however you wish.

1. Layer each 4¾"-wide coral, maroon, gold, and lavender strip with a 4¾"-wide white-on-white strip, right sides together, to make five contrasting strip pairs. From each strip pair, cut eight squares, 4¾" x 4¾" (40 total). Cut the layered squares in half diagonally. Do not separate the triangle pairs.

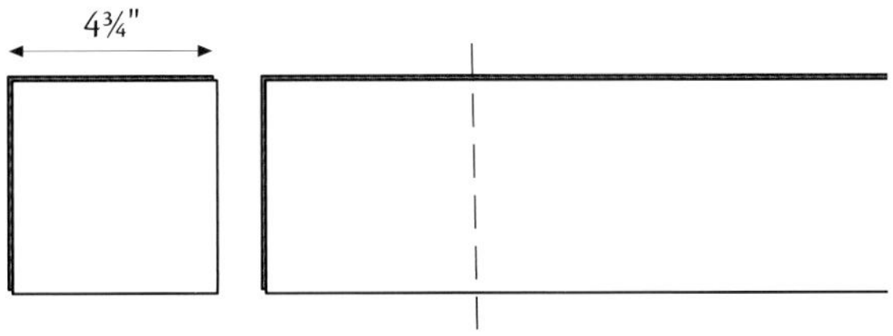

Layer and cut.

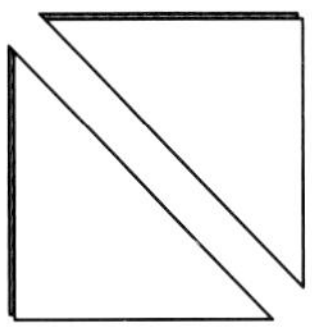
Cut.

USING LEFTOVER FABRIC

Use any leftovers to trim pillowcases, to make throw pillows or pillow shams, or as part of a pieced backing.

2. Chain stitch the triangle pairs along the long edges to make 80 half-square-triangle units.

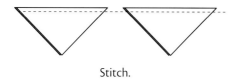

Stitch.

Make 80.

3. Cut the half-square-triangle units in half diagonally as shown. Join the resulting pieces to make 80 quarter-square-triangle units using just two fabrics in each unit. Note that two divided half-square-triangle units will make two quarter-square-triangle units, but you must "mix and match" the pieces from both units as shown.

Cut.   Mix and match.   Make 32.

Make 16.   Make 16.   Make 16.

4. Layer each 2⅝" x 25" coral, maroon, gold, and lavender strip with a 2⅝" x 25" white-on-white strip to make 10 contrasting strip pairs. From each strip pair, cut eight squares, 2⅝" x 2⅝" (80 total). Cut the layered squares in half diagonally and stitch them together along the long edges to make 160 half-square-triangle units.

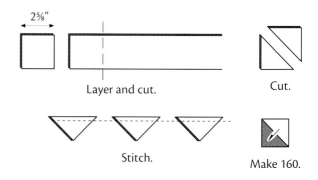

2⅝"

Layer and cut.   Cut.

Stitch.   Make 160.

5. Join the units from step 4, the 2¼" white-on-white squares and the 2¼" coral, maroon, gold, and lavender squares to make 80 units in the amounts and fabric combinations shown.

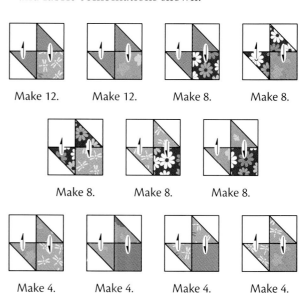

Make 12.   Make 12.   Make 8.   Make 8.

Make 8.   Make 8.   Make 8.

Make 4.   Make 4.   Make 4.   Make 4.

6. Join the units from step 3, the units from step 5, and the 4" coral, maroon, gold, and lavender squares to make 20 Golden Samovar blocks. Each block should contain just three fabrics; use the fabric combinations in the units from step 5 as a guide.

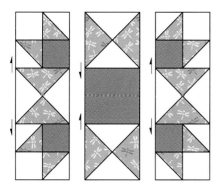

Make 20.

ASSEMBLING AND FINISHING THE QUILT

Basic instructions for borders, backing, and binding begin on page 14.

1. Join the blocks and 25 of the 2¾" x 11" lavender sashing pieces to make five block rows. Press the seam allowances toward the sashing.

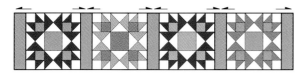

Make 5 block rows.

2. Join the remaining lavender sashing pieces and the 2¾" gold sashing squares to make six sashing rows. Press the seam allowances toward the sashing pieces.

Make 6 sashing rows.

3. Set the block rows and the sashing rows together as shown.

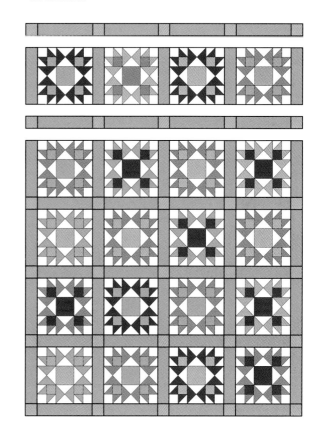

4. Add the inner border using the 1"-wide coral strips.
5. Add the outer border using the 5½"-wide lavender strips.
6. Seam the backing fabric. The seam will run lengthwise of the quilt.
7. Layer the quilt top with batting and backing; baste.
8. Hand or machine quilt.
9. Bind the quilt with the lavender strips.

GRANDMOTHER'S CHOICE

Pieced by Judy Dafoe Hopkins; quilted by Peggy Hinchey

Finished block: 7½" x 7½"
Finished quilt: 50½" x 65½"

MATERIALS

Yardage is based on 42"-wide fabric.

3 yards of light print for block backgrounds, setting squares, and inner and outer borders

1¼ yards of red print for blocks, middle border, and binding

⅝ yard of green print for blocks

3½ yards of fabric for backing

57" x 72" piece of batting

CUTTING

All cutting dimensions include ¼"-wide seam allowances. **Note:** *You may want to wait until your blocks are pieced before cutting setting squares, in case your blocks measure larger or smaller than the expected 8" x 8" (raw edge to raw edge).*

From the light print, cut:

4 strips, 3½" x 42"; crosscut *2 strips* into 34 rectangles, 2" x 3½". Leave the remaining strips uncut.

5 strips, 2⅜" x 42"; crosscut into 68 squares, 2⅜" x 2⅜". Cut the squares in half diagonally to make 136 triangles.

4 strips, 8" x 42"; crosscut into 18 squares, 8" x 8"

6 border strips, 2" x 42"

7 border strips, 4" x 42"

From the red print, cut:

5 strips, 2" x 42"; crosscut *4 strips* into 68 squares, 2" x 2". Leave the remaining strip uncut.

6 border strips, 2" x 42"

7 binding strips

From the green print, cut:

4 strips, 3⅞" x 42"; crosscut into 34 squares, 3⅞" x 3⅞". Cut the squares in half diagonally to make 68 triangles.

USING LEFTOVER FABRIC

Use the leftovers from the light print for another project or as part of a pieced backing.

MAKING THE BLOCKS

Press the seam allowances in the direction of the arrows. If there are no arrows, press the seam allowances however you wish.

1. Join the 2⅜" light triangles and the 2" red squares to make 68 unit A.

Unit A.
Make 68

2. Join the 3⅞" green triangles to the units from step 1 to make 68 unit B.

Unit B.
Make 68.

3. Join a 3½"-wide light strip to each long edge of the 2"-wide red strip to make one strip unit. From this strip unit, cut 17 segments, 2" wide.

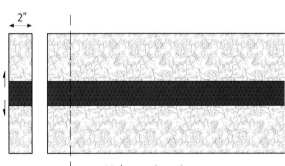

Make 1 strip unit.
Cut 17 segments.

4. Join the units from step 2, the segments from step 3, and the 2" x 3½" light rectangles to make 17 Grandmother's Choice blocks.

Make 17.

ASSEMBLING AND FINISHING THE QUILT

Basic instructions for borders, backing, and binding begin on page 14.

1. Set the pieced blocks and the 8" light squares together as shown. Press the seam allowances toward the light squares.

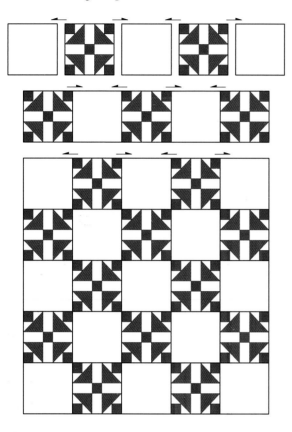

2. Add the inner border using the 2"-wide light strips.

3. Add the middle border using the remaining 2"-wide red strips.

4. Add the outer border using the 4"-wide light strips.

5. Seam the backing fabric. The seam will run crosswise of the quilt.

6. Layer the quilt top with batting and backing; baste.

7. Hand or machine quilt.

8. Bind the quilt with the red strips.

HERM'S SHIRT

Pieced and quilted by Susan Baxter; from the collection of Pete Baxter

Finished block: 9" x 9"
Finished quilt: 43" x 52"

MATERIALS

Yardage is based on 42"-wide fabric.

2⅓ yards of navy print for blocks, border, and binding
⅝ yard of cranberry print for blocks
½ yard of light print for blocks
3 yards of fabric for backing
49" x 58" piece of batting

CUTTING

All cutting dimensions include ¼"-wide seam allowance.

From the light print, cut:

4 strips, 3⅛" x 42"; crosscut *2 strips* into 24 squares, 3⅛" x 3⅛". Cut the squares in half diagonally to make 48 triangles. Leave the remaining strips uncut.

From the cranberry print, cut:

2 strips, 5⅜" x 42"; crosscut into 12 squares, 5⅜" x 5⅜". Cut the squares in half diagonally to make 24 triangles.
2 strips, 3⅛" x 42"; crosscut *1 strip* into 12 squares, 3⅛" x 3⅛". Cut the squares in half diagonally to make 24 triangles. Leave the remaining strip uncut.

From the navy print, cut:

2 strips, 5⅜" x 42"; crosscut into 12 squares, 5⅜" x 5⅜". Cut the squares in half diagonally to make 24 triangles.
2 strips, 3⅛" x 42"; crosscut *1 strip* into 12 squares, 3⅛" x 3⅛". Cut the squares in half diagonally to make 24 triangles. Leave the remaining strip uncut.
5 border strips, 8½" x 42"
6 binding strips

MAKING THE BLOCKS

For ease of construction, press seam allowances open.

1. Layer a 3⅛"-wide light strip with a 3⅛"-wide cranberry strip, right sides together, to make one contrasting strip pair. Repeat with the remaining 3⅛"-wide light strip and the 3⅛"-wide navy strip. From each strip pair, cut 12 squares, 3⅛" x 3⅛" (24 total). Cut the layered squares in half diagonally. Do not separate the triangle pairs.

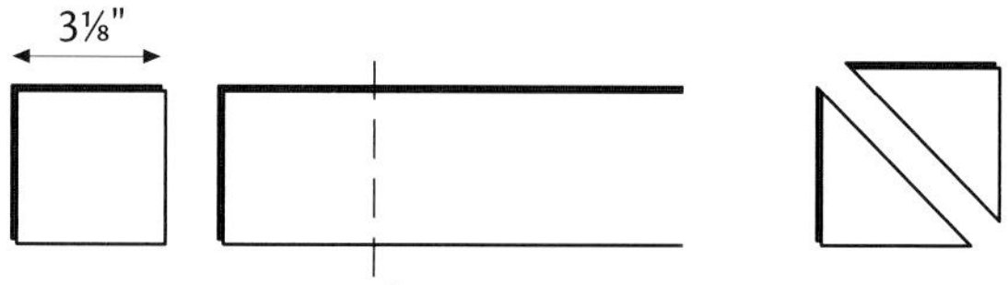

Layer and cut.   Cut.

2. Chain stitch the triangle pairs along the long edges to make 24 cranberry and 24 navy half-square-triangle units.

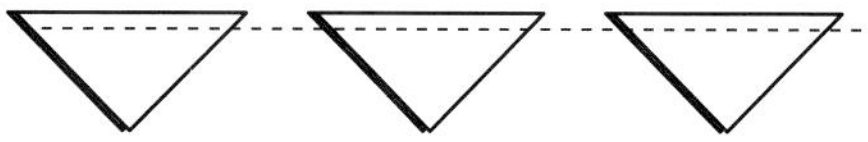

Stitch.

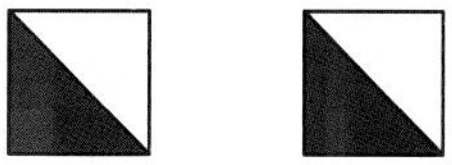

Make 24.   Make 24.

3. Join the units from step 2 and the loose 3⅛" light, cranberry, and navy triangles to make 24 unit A and 24 unit B.

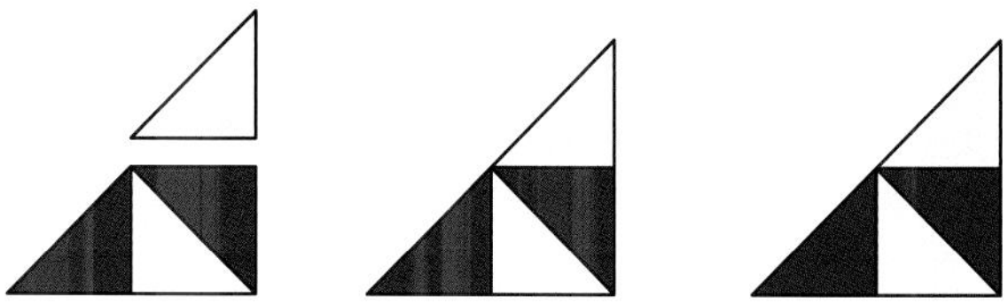

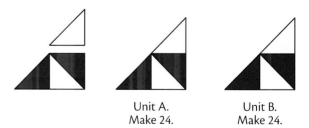

Unit A. Make 24.   Unit B. Make 24.

4. Join the 5⅜" cranberry and navy triangles to the units from step 3 to make 24 unit C and 24 unit D.

Unit C.
Make 24.

Unit D.
Make 24.

5. Join the units from step 4 to make six block A and six block B.

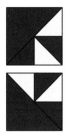  

Block A.
Make 6.

Block B.
Make 6.

ASSEMBLING AND FINISHING THE QUILT

Basic instructions for borders, backing, and binding begin on page 14.

1. Set the blocks together as shown, alternating block A and block B. Press the seam allowances in opposite directions from row to row.

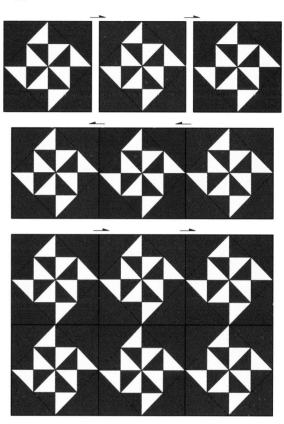

2. Add the border using the 8½"-wide navy strips.
3. Seam the backing fabric. The seam will run crosswise of the quilt.
4. Layer the quilt top with batting and backing; baste.
5. Hand or machine quilt.
6. Bind the quilt with the navy strips.

Hide and Seek

Pieced by Judy Dafoe Hopkins; quilted by Mona Norris

Finished block: 11" x 11"
Finished quilt: 63½" x 85½"

MATERIALS

Yardage is based on 42"-wide fabric.

4 yards of bright pink print for blocks, outer border, and binding

2⅞ yards of cheddar print for blocks and inner border

12 strips, exactly 3¼" wide x about 42" long, of assorted light prints for blocks*

12 strips, exactly 3¼" wide x about 42" long, of assorted dark prints for blocks*

5⅝ yards of fabric for backing

70" x 92" piece of batting

Use the same fabric more than once if you wish.

CUTTING

All cutting dimensions include ¼"-wide seam allowances.

From *each* of the 12 assorted light strips and 12 assorted dark strips, cut:

12 squares, 3¼" x 3¼" (144 light squares and 144 dark squares total; you'll use 140 light squares and 140 dark squares)

From the cheddar print, cut:

12 strips, 6⅜" x 42"; crosscut into 70 squares, 6⅜" x 6⅜"

7 border strips, 1¾" x 42"

From the pink print, cut:

12 strips, 6⅜" x 42"; crosscut into 70 squares, 6⅜" x 6⅜"

9 border strips, 3½" x 42"

8 binding strips

SAVE THE CORNERS

Seam the cut-off corners and use the resulting half-square-triangle units as part of a saw-tooth border or for another project.

MAKING THE BLOCKS

Press the seam allowances in the direction of the arrows. To avoid having to twist seam allowances on the back to make the seams butt together properly, you'll press some of the seam allowances open (as indicated by double-headed arrows).

1. Align a 3¼" dark square with the upper-left corner of a 6⅜" cheddar square, right sides together. Draw a diagonal line from corner to corner on each cheddar square and stitch on the line. Trim to leave a ¼"-wide seam allowance; press.

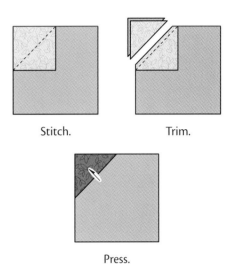

Stitch.   Trim.

Press.

2. Align a 3¼" light square with the lower-right corner of the same cheddar square, right sides together. Draw, stitch, trim, and press as before.

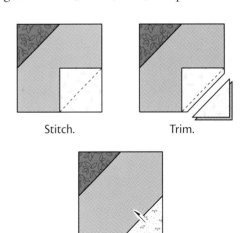

Stitch.   Trim.

Press.

3. Repeat steps 1 and 2 with the remaining cheddar and pink squares to make 70 cheddar units and 70 pink units.

Make 70.   Make 70.

4. Cut the cheddar and pink units in half diagonally as shown to make 280 triangle units.

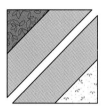 

Cut on the diagonal.

5. Join each cheddar triangle unit to a pink triangle unit to make 70 unit A and 70 unit B *exactly* as shown.

Unit A.   Unit B.
Make 70.   Make 70.

6. Join units A and B *exactly* as shown to make 35 Hide and Seek blocks. Pay particular attention to the orientation of the pink and yellow trapezoids in the block.

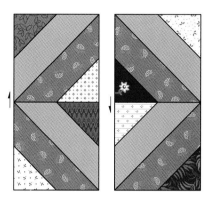

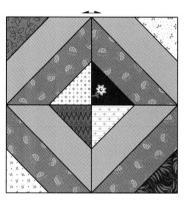

Make 35.

ASSEMBLING AND FINISHING THE QUILT

Basic instructions for borders, backing, and binding begin on page 14.

1. Set the blocks together as shown in the photo on page 84. Note that all the blocks are oriented with the cheddar trapezoids at the top. Press the seam allowances in opposite directions from row to row.

2. Add the inner border using the 1¾"-wide cheddar strips.

3. Add the outer border using the 3½"-wide pink strips.

4. Seam the backing fabric. The seam will run lengthwise of the quilt.

5. Layer the quilt top with batting and backing; baste.

6. Hand or machine quilt.

7. Bind the quilt with the pink strips.

HOMEWARD BOUND

Pieced and quilted by Willa Allison

Finished block: 7" x 7"
Finished quilt: 54½" x 65"

MATERIALS

Yardage is based on 42"-wide fabric.
3⅛ yards of light print for blocks, border, and binding
1 yard of navy print for blocks
¾ yard of rust print for blocks
3¾ yards of fabric for backing
61" x 71" piece of batting

CUTTING

All cutting dimensions include ¼"-wide seam allowances.

From the light print, cut:
10 strips, 4" x 42"; crosscut *3 strips* into 40 rectangles,
    2¼" x 4". Leave the remaining strips uncut.
5 strips, 2¼" x 42"
6 border strips, 5" x 42"
7 binding strips

From the rust print, cut:
3 strips, 4" x 42"; crosscut into 40 rectangles, 2¼" x 4"
5 strips, 2¼" x 42"

From the navy print, cut:
7 strips, 4" x 42"

MAKING THE BLOCKS

Press the seam allowances in the direction of the arrows. To avoid having to twist seam allowances on the back to make the seams butt together properly, you'll press some of the seam allowances open (as indicated by double-headed arrows). If there are no arrows, press the seam allowances however you wish.

1. Join each 2¼"-wide light print strip to a 2¼"-wide rust print strip to make five strip units. From these strip units, cut 80 segments, 2¼" wide.

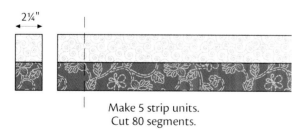

Make 5 strip units.
Cut 80 segments.

2. Join the segments from step 1 and the 2¼" x 4" light print and rust print rectangles to make 40 unit A and 40 unit B.

Unit A.
Make 40.

Unit B.
Make 40.

3. Join each 4"-wide light print strip to a 4"-wide navy strip to make seven strip units. From these strip units, cut 64 segments, 4" wide.

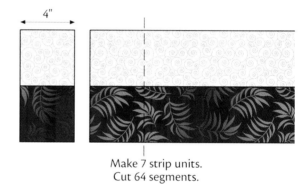

Make 7 strip units.
Cut 64 segments.

4. Join the units from step 2 and 24 of the segments from step 3 to make 12 block A, 12 block B, and eight block C.

Block A.
Make 12.

Block B.
Make 12.

Block C.
Make 8.

ASSEMBLING AND FINISHING THE QUILT

Basic instructions for borders, backing, and binding begin on page 14.

1. Join the blocks and the remaining segments from step 3 of "Making the Blocks" to make three row 1, three row 2, and two row 3 exactly as shown. Note that the A and B blocks are rotated 180° to make row 2. Press the seam allowances in opposite directions from row to row.

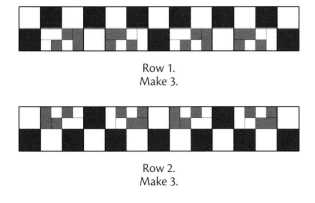

Row 1.
Make 3.

Row 2.
Make 3.

Row 3.
Make 2.

2. Join the block rows in this order, from top to bottom: 1, 2, 3, 1, 2, 3, 1, 2.

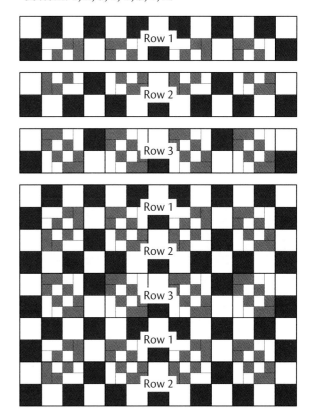

3. Add the border using the 5"-wide light print strips.
4. Seam the backing fabric. The seam will run crosswise of the quilt.
5. Layer the quilt top with batting and backing; baste.
6. Hand or machine quilt.
7. Bind the quilt with the light print strips.

JACK IN THE BOX

Pieced by Judy Dafoe Hopkins; quilted by Carol Parks

Finished block: 8" x 8"
Finished quilt: 58" x 78"

MATERIALS
Yardage is based on 42"-wide fabric.
3⅝ yards of cream print for blocks and sashing posts
3¼ yards of black fabric for blocks, sashing strips, and binding
5¼ yards of fabric for backing
64" x 84" piece of batting

CUTTING
All cutting dimensions include ¼"-wide seam allowances. **Note:** *You may want to wait until your blocks are pieced before cutting sashing pieces, in case your blocks measure larger or smaller than the expected 8½" x 8½" (raw edge to raw edge).*

From the black fabric, cut:
5 strips, 8½" x 42"; crosscut *3 strips* into 48 sashing rectangles, 2½" x 8½". Leave the remaining strips uncut.
9 strips, 4½" x 42"; crosscut into 144 rectangles, 2½" x 4½"
1 strip, 2½" x 42"; crosscut into 2 sashing rectangles, 2½" x 8½"
8 binding strips

From the cream print, cut:
3 strips, 8½" x 42"; crosscut into 24 rectangles, 4½" x 8½"
9 strips, 4½" x 42"; crosscut into 72 squares, 4½" x 4½"
21 strips, 2½" x 42"; crosscut *19 strips* into 291 squares, 2½" x 2½". Leave the remaining strips uncut.

MAKING THE BLOCKS
Press the seam allowances in the direction of the arrows. If there are no arrows, press the seam allowances however you wish.

1. Align 2½" cream squares with the left-hand corners of the 2½" x 4½" black rectangles, right sides together. Draw a diagonal line from corner to corner on each of the cream squares as shown and stitch on the lines. Trim to leave ¼"-wide seam allowances; press.

Stitch.   Trim.   Make 144.

2. Align 2½" cream squares with the right-hand corners of 72 of the units from step 1, right sides together. Draw diagonal lines from corner to corner as shown and stitch on the lines. Trim and press as above.

Stitch.   Trim.   Make 72.

3. Align *all but three* of the remaining 2½" cream squares with the right-hand corners of the remaining units from step 1, right sides together. Paying careful attention to the direction of the lines, draw diagonal lines from corner to corner as shown and stitch on the lines. Trim and press as above.

Stitch.   Trim.   Make 72.

SAVE THE CORNERS
Seam the cut-off corners and use the resulting half-square-triangle units as part of a sawtooth border or for another project.

4. Join the units from steps 2 and 3 to make 72 units.

Make 72.

5. Join the units from step 4, the 4½" cream squares, and the 4½" x 8½" cream rectangles to make 24 block A, 12 block B, and 12 block C *exactly* as shown.

  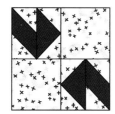

Block A.
Make 24.

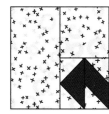 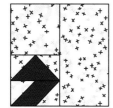

Block B.
Make 12.

Block C.
Make 12.

ASSEMBLING AND FINISHING THE QUILT

Basic instructions for borders, backing, and binding begin on page 14.

1. Join the 2½"-wide cream strips and the 8½"-wide black strips to make two strip units. From these strip units, cut 32 segments, 2½" wide.

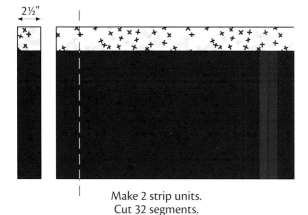

Make 2 strip units.
Cut 32 segments.

2. Join three of the 2½" x 8½" black rectangles and the three remaining 2½" cream squares to make three units identical to the segments you cut in step 1, for a total of 35 segments.

3. Join the blocks and 40 of the 2½" x 8½" black sashing rectangles to make two row 1, three row 2, and three row 3 *exactly* as shown. Press the seam allowances toward the sashing rectangles.

Row 1.
Make 2.

Row 2.
Make 3.

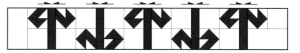

Row 3.
Make 3.

4. Join the segments from steps 1 and 2 and the remaining 2½" x 8½" black sashing rectangles to make seven sashing rows. Press the seam allowances toward the sashing rectangles.

Make 7.

5. Set the block rows and the sashing rows together as shown in the photo on page 90.
6. Seam the backing fabric. The seam will run lengthwise of the quilt.
7. Layer the quilt top with batting and backing; baste.
8. Hand or machine quilt.
9. Bind the quilt with the black strips.

JAPANESE SAMPLER

Pieced by Judy Forrest; quilted by Sandy Fruehling

Finished block: 5½" x 5½"
Finished quilt: 54½" x 69½"

MATERIALS

Yardage is based on 42"-wide fabric.

9 fat quarters (18" x 20") of assorted white-on-black and black-on-black prints for sashing strips

63 squares, 6" x 6", of assorted Japanese-style prints for blocks*

½ yard of red print for sashing squares

⅝ yard of black print for binding

4 yards of fabric for backing

61" x 76" piece of batting

Use the same fabric more than once, if you wish.

CUTTING

All cutting dimensions include ¼"-wide seam allowances.

From *each* of the 9 fat quarters, cut:
2 strips, 6" x 21" (18 total); crosscut into 142 sashing rectangles, 2½" x 6"

From the red print, cut:
5 strips, 2½" x 42"; crosscut into 80 squares, 2½" x 2½"

From the black print, cut:
7 binding strips

USING LEFTOVER FABRIC

Use the leftovers from the fat quarters for another project, or as part of a pieced backing.

ASSEMBLING AND FINISHING THE QUILT

Basic instructions for backing and binding begin on page 14.

1. Randomly join 72 of the assorted 2½" x 6" sashing rectangles and the 6" Japanese print squares to make nine block rows. Press the seam allowances toward the sashing rectangles.

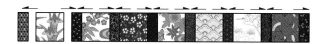

Make 9.

2. Randomly join the remaining sashing rectangles and the 2½" red squares to make 10 sashing rows. Press the seam allowances toward the sashing rectangles.

Make 10.

3. Set the block rows and the sashing rows together as shown in the photo on page 93.
4. Seam the backing fabric. The seam will run crosswise of the quilt.
5. Layer the quilt top with batting and backing; baste.
6. Hand or machine quilt.
7. Bind the quilt with the black strips.

Jordan River

Pieced and quilted by Elise Rose

Finished block: 7" x 7"
Finished quilt: 61" x 75"

MATERIALS

Yardage is based on 42"-wide fabric.

4 yards of oatmeal solid fabric for blocks, borders, and binding

16 rectangles, 13" x 21", of assorted medium and dark prints for blocks. Use blacks, navy blues, browns, tans, and golds.*

⅓ yard of black print for middle border**

5 yards of fabric for backing

67" x 81" piece of batting

Use the same fabric more than once, if you wish.

**Use one of the fabrics you used for the blocks or a completely different fabric.*

CUTTING

All cutting dimensions include ¼"-wide seam allowances.

From the oatmeal solid fabric, cut:

7 strips, 5½" x 42"; crosscut into 126 rectangles, 2" x 5½"

2 strips, 12" x 42"; crosscut into 32 strips, 2" x 12"

7 border strips, 1¾" x 42"

8 border strips, 4½" x 42"

8 binding strips

From *each* of the 16 assorted medium and dark print pieces, cut:

2 strips, 4½" x 21" (32 total); crosscut into 126 squares, 4½" x 4½". Cut the squares in half diagonally to make 252 triangles.

1 strip, 2½" x 12" (16 total)

From the black print, cut:

7 border strips, 1¼" x 42"

MAKING THE BLOCKS

Press the seam allowances in the direction of the arrows. If there are no arrows, press the seam allowances however you wish.

1. Join two 2" x 12" oatmeal strips to each 2½" x 12" medium or dark strip to make 16 strip units. From these strip units, cut 63 segments, 2½" wide.

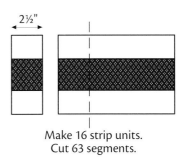

Make 16 strip units.
Cut 63 segments.

2. Join the segments from step 1 and the 2" x 5½" oatmeal rectangles to make 63 unit A.

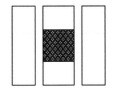

Unit A.
Make 63.

3. Randomly join 4½" medium and dark triangles to the units from step 2 to make 63 Jordan River blocks (see "Stitching Tips for Square-in-a-Square Units" on page 12). Trim the blocks to 7½" x 7½" as needed, leaving ¼" outside the oatmeal points for seams.

Make 63.

ASSEMBLING AND FINISHING THE QUILT

Basic instructions for borders, backing, and binding begin on page 14.

1. Set the blocks together as shown. Press the seam allowances in opposite directions from row to row.

2. Add the inner border using the 1¾"-wide oatmeal strips.

3. Add the middle border using the 1¼"-wide black strips.

4. Add the outer border using the 4½"-wide oatmeal strips.

5. Seam the backing fabric. The seam will run lengthwise of the quilt.

6. Layer the quilt top with batting and backing; baste.

7. Hand or machine quilt.

8. Bind the quilt with the oatmeal strips.

LADY OF THE LAKE

Pieced and quilted by Blanche Smith; from the collection of Lucy Jean Smith

Finished block: 10½" x 10½"
Finished quilt: 63" x 73½"

MATERIALS

Yardage is based on 42"-wide fabric.
4⅛ yards of muslin for blocks and binding
3½ yards of sky blue solid fabric for blocks
4¼ yards of fabric for backing
69" x 80" piece of batting

CUTTING

All cutting dimensions include ¼"-wide seam allowances.

From the muslin, cut:
5 strips, 7⅞" x 42"
28 strips, 2⅝" x 42"
8 binding strips

From the sky blue solid fabric, cut:
5 strips, 7⅞" x 42"
28 strips, 2⅝" x 42"

MAKING THE BLOCKS

Press the seam allowances in the direction of the arrows.

1. Layer each 7⅞"-wide muslin strip with a 7⅞"-wide sky blue strip, right sides together, to make five contrasting strip pairs. From these strip pairs, cut 21 squares, 7⅞" x 7⅞". Cut the layered squares in half diagonally. Do not separate the triangle pairs.

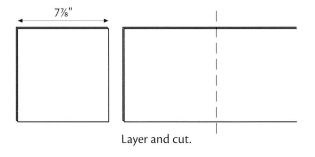

Layer and cut.

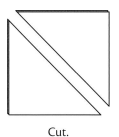

Cut.

2. Chain stitch the triangle pairs along the long edges to make 42 large half-square-triangle units.

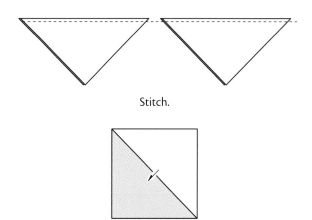

Stitch.

Make 42.

3. Layer each 2⅝"-wide muslin strip with a 2⅝"-wide sky blue strip to make 28 contrasting strip pairs. From these strip pairs, cut 420 squares, 2⅝" x 2⅝". Cut the layered squares in half diagonally and chain stitch along the long edges to make 840 small half-square-triangle units.

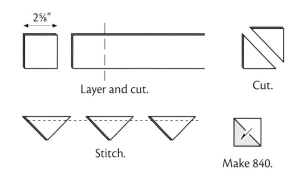

2⅝"

Layer and cut.

Cut.

Stitch.

Make 840.

4. Join the units from steps 2 and 3 to make 42 Lady of the Lake blocks.

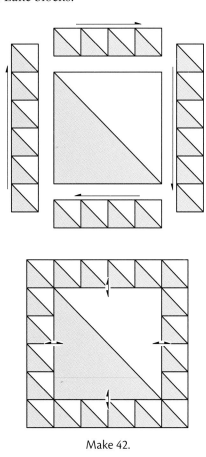

Make 42.

ASSEMBLING AND FINISHING THE QUILT

Basic instructions for borders, backing, and binding begin on page 14.

1. Set the blocks together as shown. Note that the blocks should be oriented with all the sky blue triangles at the bottom left. Press the seam allowances in opposite directions from row to row.

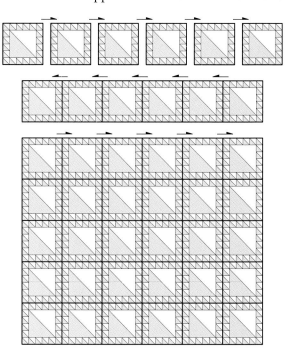

2. Seam the backing fabric. The seam will run crosswise of the quilt.
3. Layer the quilt top with batting and backing; baste.
4. Hand or machine quilt.
5. Bind the quilt with the muslin strips.

LOG JAM

Pieced and quilted by George Taylor

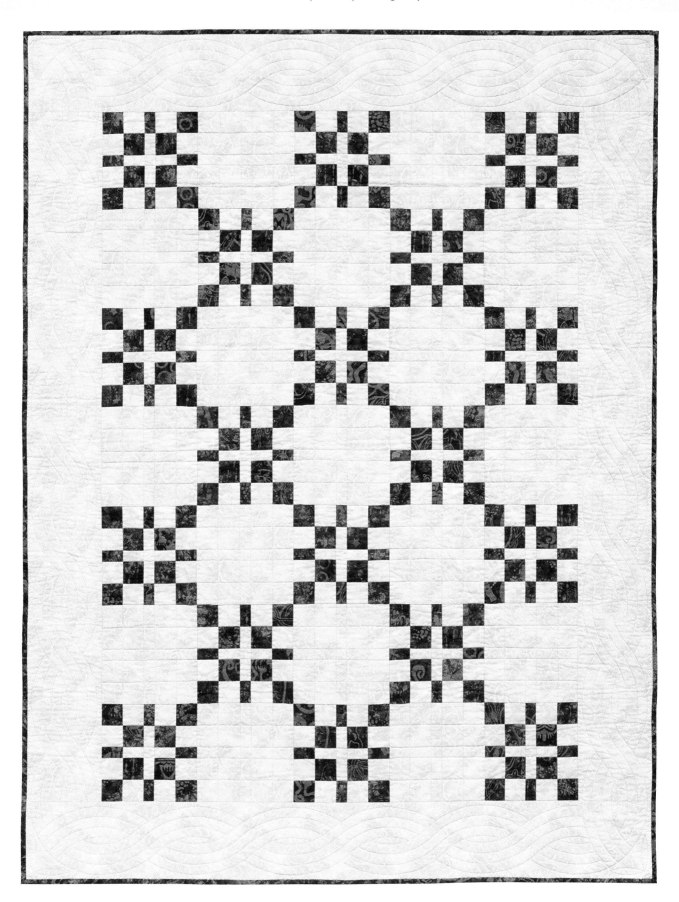

Finished block: 9" x 9"
Finished quilt: 59½" x 77½"

MATERIALS

Yardage is based on 42"-wide fabric.

4⅔ yards of aqua print for block backgrounds, setting squares, and border

1⅞ yards of teal print for blocks and binding

5⅛ yards of fabric for backing

66" x 84" piece of batting

CUTTING

All cutting dimensions include ¼"-wide seam allowances. **Note:** *You may want to wait until your blocks are pieced before cutting setting squares, in case your pieced blocks measure larger or smaller than the expected 9½" x 9½" (raw edge to raw edge).*

From the teal print, cut:

14 strips, 2½" x 42"

3 strips, 1½" x 42"

8 binding strips

From the aqua print, cut:

5 strips, 9½" x 42"; crosscut into 17 setting squares, 9½" x 9½"

1 strip, 5½" x 42"

12 strips, 2½" x 42"

3 strips, 1½" x 42"

8 border strips, 7¾" x 42"

MAKING THE BLOCKS

Press the seam allowances in the direction of the arrows. If there are no arrows, press the seam allowances however you wish.

1. Join 1½"- and 2½"-wide teal strips and 2½"-wide aqua strips as shown to make three strip unit A. From these strip units, cut 36 segments, 2½" wide.

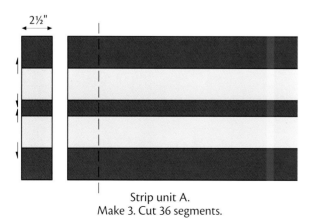

2½"

Strip unit A.
Make 3. Cut 36 segments.

2. Join 1½"- and 2½"-wide aqua strips and 2½"-wide teal strips as shown to make three strip unit B. From these strip units, cut 36 segments, 2½" wide.

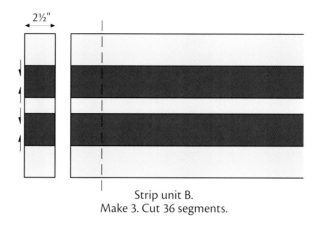

2½"

Strip unit B.
Make 3. Cut 36 segments.

3. Join 2½"-wide teal strips and the 5½"-wide aqua strip to make one strip unit C. From this strip unit, cut 18 segments, 1½" wide.

1½"

Strip unit C.
Make 1. Cut 18 segments.

4. Join the A, B, and C strip-unit segments to make 18 Log Jam blocks.

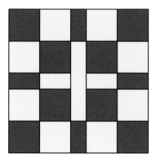

Make 18.

ASSEMBLING AND FINISHING THE QUILT

Basic instructions for borders, backing, and binding begin on page 14.

1. Set the pieced blocks and the 9½" aqua setting squares together as shown. Press the seam allowances toward the setting squares.

2. Add the border using the 7¾"-wide aqua strips.
3. Seam the backing fabric. The seam will run lengthwise of the quilt.
4. Layer the quilt top with batting and backing; baste.
5. Hand or machine quilt.
6. Bind the quilt with the teal strips.

LOIS' STAR

Pieced by Beverly Fugazzi; quilted by Lisa Cavanaugh

Finished block: 13¾" x 13¾"
Finished quilt: 23¼" x 50¾"

MATERIALS

Yardage is based on 42"-wide fabric.

⅞ yard of gold print for blocks and outer border
⅝ yard of light print for block backgrounds
⅝ yard of bright blue print 1 for blocks and binding
¼ yard of bright blue print 2 for inner border
⅜ yard of black print for blocks
1¾ yards of fabric for backing
30" x 57" piece of batting

CUTTING

All cutting dimensions include ¼"-wide seam allowances.

From the light print, cut:

1 strip, 7½" x 42". From one end of this strip, cut 3 squares, 7½" x 7½". Cut the squares into quarters diagonally to make 12 triangles. From the remaining piece of the strip, cut 3 squares, 4¼" x 4¼".
1 strip, 4⅝" x 42"
2 strips, 2⅛" x 42"
1 strip, 1¾" x 42"; crosscut into 12 squares, 1¾" x 1¾"

From the gold print, cut:

1 strip, 4⅝" x 42"
5 border strips, 4¾" x 42"

From the black print, cut:

1 strip, 5" x 42"; crosscut into 3 squares, 5" x 5". Cut the squares into quarters diagonally to make 12 triangles.
3 strips, 2⅛" x 42"; crosscut *1 strip* into 12 squares, 2⅛" x 2⅛". Cut the squares in half diagonally to make 24 triangles. Leave the remaining strips uncut.

From bright blue print 1, cut:

1 strip, 5" x 42"; crosscut into 6 squares, 5" x 5". Cut the squares into quarters diagonally to make 24 triangles.
5 binding strips

From bright blue print 2, cut:

4 border strips, 1" x 42"

MAKING THE BLOCKS

Press the seam allowances in the direction of the arrows. If there are no arrows, press the seam allowances however you wish.

1. Layer the 4⅝"-wide light strip with the 4⅝"-wide gold strip, right sides together, to make a contrasting strip pair. From this strip pair, cut six squares, 4⅝" x 4⅝". Cut the layered squares in half diagonally. Do not separate the triangle pairs.

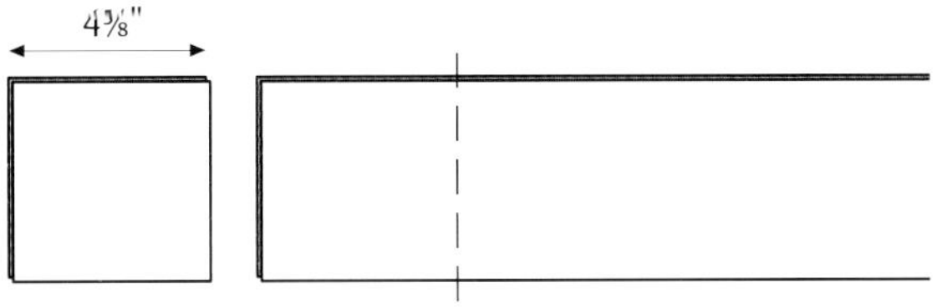

Layer and cut.

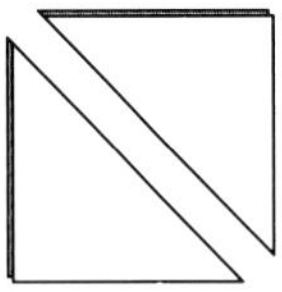
Cut.

2. Chain stitch the triangle pairs along the long edges to make 12 half-square-triangle units.

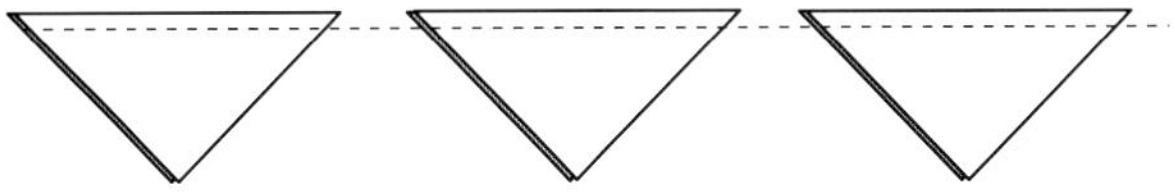
Stitch.

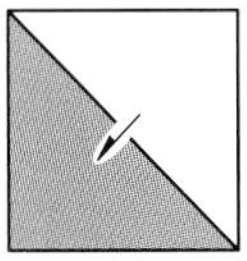
Make 12.

3. Layer the 2⅛"-wide light and black strips to make two contrasting strip pairs. From these strip pairs, cut 24 squares, 2⅛" x 2⅛". Cut the layered squares in half diagonally and chain stitch along the long edges to make 48 half-square-triangle units.

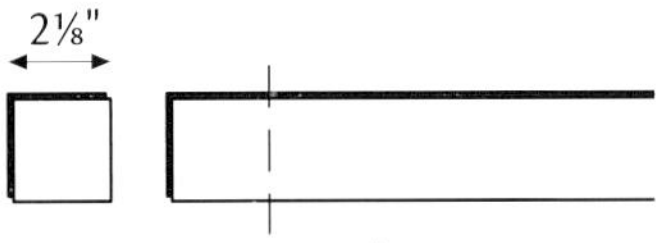

Layer and cut.

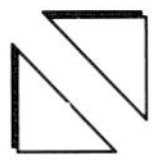
Cut.

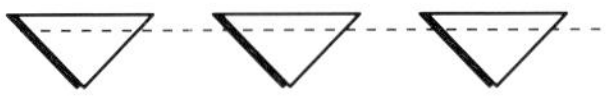
Stitch.

Make 48.

4. Join the units from step 3, the loose 2⅛" black triangles, and the 1¾" light squares to make 12 unit A and 12 unit B.

Unit A.
Make 12.

Unit B.
Make 12.

5. Join the units from steps 2 and 4 to make 12 unit C.

Unit C.
Make 12.

6. Join 5" triangles of bright blue 1 to the units from step 5 to make 12 unit D.

Unit D.
Make 12.

7. Join 7½" light triangles to six of the D units to make 6 unit E.

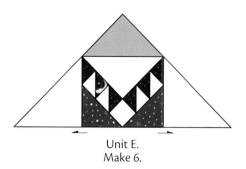

Unit E.
Make 6.

8. Join 5" black triangles to the 4¼" light squares to make three unit F (see "Stitching Tips for Square-in-a-Square Units" on page 12).

Unit F.
Make 3.

9. Join the F units and the remaining D units to make three unit G.

Unit G.
Make 3.

10. Join units E and G to make three Lois' Star blocks.

Make 3.

ASSEMBLING AND FINISHING THE QUILT

Basic instructions for borders, backing, and binding begin on page 14.

1. Set the blocks together as shown in the photo on page 104.
2. Add the inner border using the 1"-wide strips of bright blue 2.
3. Add the outer border using the 4¾"-wide gold strips.
4. Layer the quilt top with batting and backing; baste.
5. Hand or machine quilt.
6. Bind the quilt with the bright blue 1 strips.

LOST SHIP

Pieced by Cherrie VanElverdinghe; quilted by Carol Parks

Finished block: 11¼" x 11¼"
Finished quilt: 57½" x 68¾"

MATERIALS

Yardage is based on 42"-wide fabric.

3¾ yards of light blue print for blocks and inner and outer borders

½ yard of medium blue print for middle border

20 rectangles, 12" x 15", of assorted medium and/or dark ocean-colored prints for blocks. Use blues, greens, and blue-greens.*

⅝ yard of dotted blue print for binding

4 yards of fabric for backing

64" x 75" piece of batting

Use the same fabric more than once, if you wish.

CUTTING

All cutting dimensions include ¼"-wide seam allowances.

From the light blue print, cut:

3 strips, 15" x 42"; crosscut into 40 rectangles, 2¾" x 15"

3 strips, 11" x 42"; crosscut into 20 rectangles, 4⅝" x 11"

6 border strips, 2¾" x 42"

8 border strips, 3½" x 42"

From *each* of the 20 assorted ocean-colored prints, cut:

2 strips, 2¾" x 15" (40 total)

1 rectangle, 4⅝" x 11" (20 total)

From the medium blue print, cut:

8 border strips, 1½" x 42"

From the dotted blue print, cut:

7 binding strips

MAKING THE BLOCKS

For ease of construction, press seam allowances open.

1. Layer each 4⅝" x 11" light blue rectangle with a 4⅝" x 11" ocean-colored rectangle, right sides together, to make 20 contrasting strip pairs. From *each* strip pair, cut two squares, 4⅝" x 4⅝" (40 total). Cut the layered squares in half diagonally. Do not separate the triangle pairs.

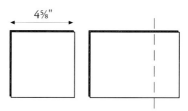

Layer and cut.

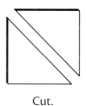

Cut.

2. Chain stitch the triangle pairs along the long edges to make 80 large half-square-triangle units.

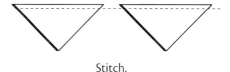

Stitch.

Make 80.

3. Layer the 2¾" x 15" light blue and ocean-colored rectangles to make 40 contrasting strip pairs. From *each* strip pair, cut five squares, 2¾" x 2¾" (200

total). Cut the layered squares in half diagonally and chain stitch along the long edges to make 400 small half-square-triangle units.

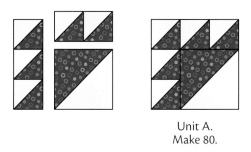

Layer and cut.

Cut.

Stitch.

Make 400.

4. Join the units from steps 2 and 3 to make 80 unit A using just one ocean-colored print in each unit.

Unit A.
Make 80.

5. Randomly join the units from step 4 to make 20 Lost Ship blocks.

Make 20.

ASSEMBLING AND FINISHING THE QUILT

Basic instructions for borders, backing, and binding begin on page 14.

1. Set the blocks together as shown below. Press the seam allowances in opposite directions from row to row.

2. Add the inner border using the 2¾"-wide light blue strips.
3. Add the middle border using the 1½"-wide medium blue strips.
4. Add the outer border using the 3½"-wide light blue strips.
5. Seam the backing fabric. The seam will run crosswise of the quilt.
6. Layer the quilt top with batting and backing; baste.
7. Hand or machine quilt.
8. Bind the quilt with the dotted blue print strips.

MT. FAIRWEATHER

Pieced by Janet Strait Gorton; quilted by Norma Kindred

Finished block: 12" x 12"
Finished quilt: 61½" x 73½"

MATERIALS

Yardage is based on 42"-wide fabric.

2 yards of medium green print for outer border and binding

½ yard of dark green print for inner border

20 strips, 3½" x 42", of assorted light prints for blocks. Use light or light-medium pinks, lavenders, aquas, and creams.*

20 strips, 3½" x 42", of assorted dark-medium and dark green prints for blocks*

4⅛ yards of fabric for backing

68" x 80" piece of batting

Use the same fabric more than once, if you wish.

CUTTING

All cutting dimensions include ¼"-wide seam allowances.

From *each* of the 20 assorted light strips, cut:

4 rectangles, 3½" x 6½" (80 total)

4 squares, 3½" x 3½" (80 total)

From *each* of the 20 assorted green strips, cut:

4 rectangles, 3½" x 6½" (80 total)

4 squares, 3½" x 3½" (80 total)

From the dark green print, cut:

7 border strips, 2" x 42"

From the medium green print, cut:

8 border strips, 5¾" x 42"

8 binding strips

SAVE THE CORNERS

Seam the cut-off corners and use the resulting half-square-triangle units as part of a sawtooth border or for another project.

MAKING THE BLOCKS

Press the seam allowances in the direction of the arrows. To avoid having to twist seam allowances on the back to make the seams butt together properly, you'll press some of the seam allowances open (as indicated by double-headed arrows).

1. Randomly align 3½" green squares with the left-hand corners of the 3½" x 6½" light rectangles, right sides together. Draw a diagonal line from corner to corner on each green square as shown and stitch on the lines to make 80 unit A. Trim to leave ¼"-wide seam allowances; press.

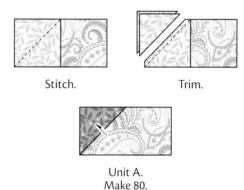

Stitch.   Trim.

Unit A.
Make 80.

2. Randomly align 3½" light squares with the left-hand corners of the 3½" x 6½" green rectangles, right sides together. Draw, stitch, trim, and press as before to make 80 unit B.

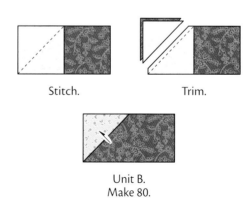

Stitch.   Trim.

Unit B.
Make 80.

3. Randomly join the A and B units to make 80 unit C.

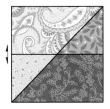

Unit C.
Make 80.

4. Randomly join the C units to make 20 Mt. Fairweather blocks.

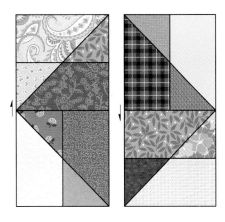

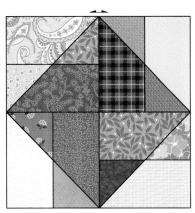

Make 20.

ALTERNATE SETTING CHOICES

Because the C units are divided diagonally into light and dark sections, you could arrange them in any Log Cabin setting, such as Streak of Lightning, Barn Raising, or Straight Furrows, instead of joining them to make Mt. Fairweather blocks.

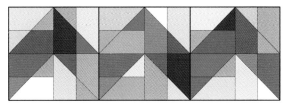

Streak of Lightning

ASSEMBLING AND FINISHING THE QUILT

Basic instructions for borders, backing, and binding begin on page 14.

1. Set the blocks together as shown in the photo on page 110. Press the seam allowances in opposite directions from row to row.
2. Add the inner border using the 2"-wide dark green strips.
3. Add the outer border using the 5¾"-wide medium green strips.
4. Seam the backing fabric. The seam will run crosswise of the quilt.
5. Layer the quilt top with batting and backing; baste.
6. Hand or machine quilt.
7. Bind the quilt with the medium green strips.

North Wind

Pieced by Marilyn Fisher; quilted by Nancy Goldsworthy

Finished block: 15" x 15"
Finished quilt: 63½" x 78½"

MATERIALS

Yardage is based on 42"-wide fabric.

2⅞ yards of medium-scale red print for outer border and binding

2 yards of cream print for blocks

¼ yard *each* of 6 assorted brown prints for blocks (don't use fat quarters)

¾ yard of red print for blocks

⅜ yard of brown print for inner border

5¼ yards of fabric for backing

70" x 85" piece of batting

CUTTING

All cutting dimensions include ¼"-wide seam allowances.

From the cream print, cut:

4 strips, 5⅞" x 42"; crosscut into 24 squares, 5⅞" x 5⅞". Cut the squares in half diagonally to make 48 triangles.

12 strips, 3⅜" x 42"; crosscut *5 strips* into 48 squares, 3⅜" x 3⅜". Cut the squares in half diagonally to make 96 triangles. Leave the remaining strips uncut.

From *each* of the 6 assorted brown prints, cut:

2 strips, 3⅜" x 42" (12 total); crosscut *5 strips* (each one a different fabric) into 48 squares, 3⅜" x 3⅜". Cut the squares in half diagonally to make 96 triangles. Leave the remaining strips uncut.

From the red print, cut:

4 strips, 5⅞" x 42"; crosscut into 24 squares, 5⅞" x 5⅞". Cut the squares in half diagonally to make 48 triangles.

From the brown print for inner border, cut:

7 strips, 1½" x 42"

From the medium-scale red print, cut:

8 border strips, 8¾" x 42"

8 binding strips

MAKING THE BLOCKS

Press the seam allowances in the direction of the arrows. To avoid having to twist seam allowances on the back to make the seams butt together properly, you'll press some of the seam allowances open (as indicated by double-headed arrows).

1. Layer each 3⅜"-wide cream strip with a 3⅜"-wide brown strip, right sides together, to make seven contrasting strip pairs. From these strip pairs, cut 72 squares, 3⅜" x 3⅜". Cut the layered squares in half diagonally. Do not separate the triangle pairs.

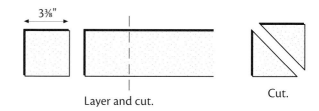

Layer and cut.　　　　Cut.

2. Chain stitch the triangle pairs along the long edges to make 144 half-square-triangle units.

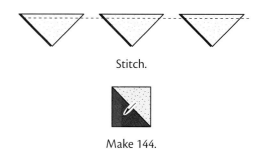

Stitch.

Make 144.

3. Join the units from step 2 and the loose 3⅜" cream and brown triangles to make 48 unit A and 96 unit B. In the B units, combine the brown prints at random.

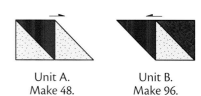

Unit A.
Make 48.

Unit B.
Make 96.

4. Join the remaining 3⅜" cream triangles to any 48 of the B units to make 48 unit C.

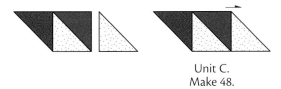

Unit C.
Make 48.

5. Randomly join units A, B, and C to make 48 unit D.

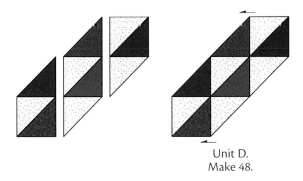

Unit D.
Make 48.

6. Join the units from step 5 and the 5⅞" cream and red triangles to make 48 unit E *exactly* as shown.

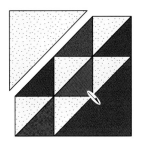 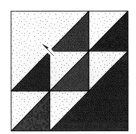

Unit E.
Make 48.

7. Randomly join the units from step 6, orienting them *exactly* as shown to make 12 North Wind blocks.

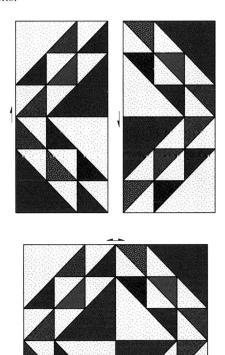

Make 12.

ASSEMBLING AND FINISHING THE QUILT

Basic instructions for borders, backing, and binding begin on page 14.

1. Set the blocks together as shown in the photo on page 113. Note that the blocks are oriented with the cream corners at the upper left and lower right. Press the seam allowances in opposite directions from row to row.
2. Add the inner border using the 1½"-wide brown strips.
3. Add the outer border using the 8¾"-wide medium-scale red print strips.
4. Seam the backing fabric. The seam will run lengthwise of the quilt.
5. Layer the quilt top with batting and backing; baste.
6. Hand or machine quilt.
7. Bind the quilt with the medium-scale red print strips.

OLD MAID'S PUZZLE

Pieced and quilted by Julie Wilkinson Kimberlin

Finished blocks:
 Block A: 4" x 4"
 Blocks B and E: 8" x 8"
 Blocks C and D: 4" x 8"
Finished quilt: 61½" x 77½"

MATERIALS

Yardage is based on 42"-wide fabric.

½ yard *each* of 6 assorted purple prints for blocks
2¼ yards of purple print for outer border and binding
1⅞ yards of taupe print for blocks
1 yard of light print for block backgrounds
¼ yard of purple striped fabric for inner border
5⅛ yards of fabric for backing
68" x 84" piece of batting

CUTTING

All cutting dimensions include ¼"-wide seam allowances.

From the taupe print, cut:

6 strips, 4½" x 42"; crosscut into 92 rectangles, 2½" x 4½"
3 strips, 5¼" x 42"; crosscut into 21 squares, 5¼" x 5¼". Cut the squares into quarters diagonally to make 84 triangles (you'll use 82). Pin a note that says "5¼" to these triangles.
2 strips, 3⅜" x 42"; crosscut into 18 squares, 3⅜" x 3⅜"
3 strips, 2⅞" x 42"; crosscut into:
 6 rectangles, 2⅞" x 10"
 14 squares, 2⅞" x 2⅞"; cut the squares in half diagonally to make 28 triangles. Pin a note that says "2⅞" to these triangles.

From *each* of the 6 assorted purple prints, cut:

1 strip, 2⅞" x 42" (6 total). From one end of *each* strip, cut 1 rectangle, 2⅞" x 10"; set it aside. From the remaining piece of each strip, cut 6 squares, 2⅞" x 2⅞" (36 total). Cut the squares in half diagonally to make 72 triangles.
1 strip, 4⅞" x 42" (6 total); crosscut *each* strip into 8 squares, 4⅞" x 4⅞" (48 total). Cut the squares in half diagonally to make 96 triangles.
2 strips, 2½" x 42" (12 total); crosscut into 184 squares, 2½" x 2½"

From the light print, cut:

6 strips, 2½" x 42"; crosscut into 96 squares, 2½" x 2½"
3 strips, 4½" x 42"; crosscut into:
 17 squares, 4½" x 4½"
 14 rectangles, 2½" x 4½"

From the purple striped fabric, cut:

6 border strips, 1¼" x 42"

From the purple print for border and binding, cut:

8 border strips, 6½" x 42"
8 binding strips

MAKING THE BLOCKS

Press the seam allowances in the direction of the arrows. If there are no arrows, press the seam allowances however you wish.

1. Layer each 2⅞" x 10" taupe rectangle with a 2⅞" x 10" purple rectangle, right sides together, to make six contrasting pairs. From these pairs, cut 16 squares, 2⅞" x 2⅞". Cut the layered squares in half diagonally. Do not separate the triangle pairs.

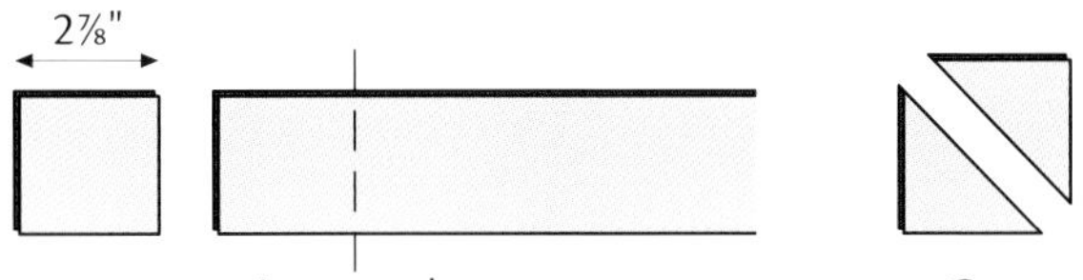

Layer and cut. Cut.

2. Chain stitch the triangle pairs along the long edges to make 32 half-square-triangle units.

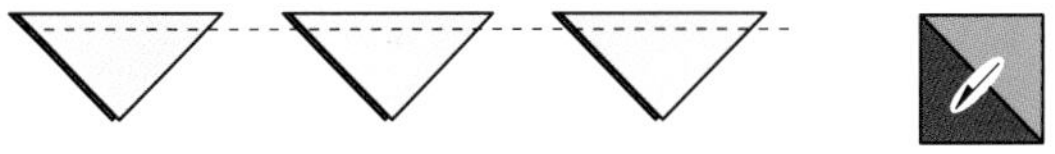

Stitch. Make 32.

3. Join 2⅞" taupe triangles to four of the units from step 2. Join any four 4⅞" purple triangles to these units to make four block A.

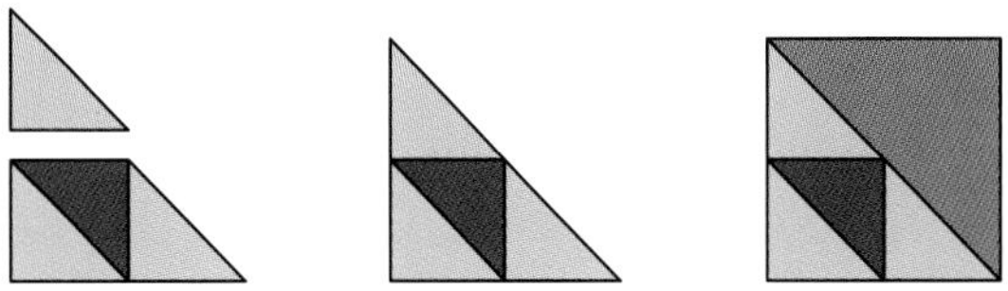

Block A.
Make 4.

4. Refer to "Stitching Tips for Square-in-a-Square Units" on page 12. Randomly join 2⅞" purple triangles to the 3⅜" taupe squares to make 18 units. Next, join 5¼" taupe triangles to the corners of these units. Finally, randomly join 4⅞" purple triangles to the corners of these units to make 18 block B.

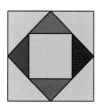

Block B.
Make 18.

5. Align randomly selected 2½" purple squares with the left-hand corners of the 2½" x 4½" taupe rectangles, right sides together. Draw a diagonal line from corner to corner on each of the purple squares as shown and stitch on the lines. Trim to leave ¼"-wide seam allowances; press.

Stitch. Trim. Make 92.

6. Align the remaining 2½" purple squares with the right-hand corners of the units from step 5, combining the fabrics at random and placing right sides together. Draw, stitch, trim, and press as before.

Stitch. Trim. Make 92.

SAVE THE CORNERS
Seam the cut-off corners and use the resulting half-square-triangle units as part of a sawtooth border or for another project.

7. Join 2⅞" and 5¼" taupe triangles to any 10 of the units from step 6. Randomly join 4⅞" purple triangles to these units to make 10 block C.

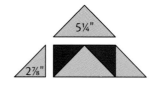

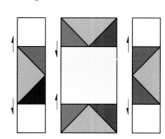

Block C.
Make 10.

8. Randomly join the remaining units from step 1, 14 of the units from step 6, 28 of the 2½" light squares, and the 2½" x 4½" light rectangles to make 14 block D.

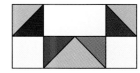

Block D.
Make 14.

9. Randomly join the remaining units from step 6, the remaining 2½" light squares, and the 4½" light squares to make 17 block E.

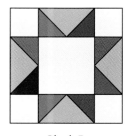

Block E.
Make 17.

ASSEMBLING AND FINISHING THE QUILT

Basic instructions for borders, backing, and binding begin on page 14.

1. Join the blocks to make two row 1, four row 2, and three row 3 as shown.

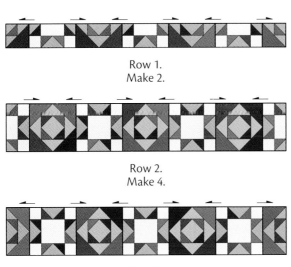

Row 1.
Make 2.

Row 2.
Make 4.

Row 3.
Make 3.

2. Join the block rows in this order, from top to bottom: 1, 2, 3, 2, 3, 2, 3, 2, 1. (The bottom row is turned upside down.)
3. Add the inner border using the 1¼"-wide purple striped strips.

4. Add the outer border using the 6½"-wide purple print strips.

5. Seam the backing fabric. The seam will run lengthwise of the quilt.
6. Layer the quilt top with batting and backing; baste.
7. Hand or machine quilt.
8. Bind the quilt with the purple print strips.

OLD MAID'S RAMBLER

Pieced by Anne Richardson; quilted by Julie Wilkinson Kimberlin

Finished block: 12" x 12"
Finished quilt: 60" x 72"

MATERIALS

Yardage is based on 42"-wide fabric.
2⅛ yards of deep blue print for blocks and binding
1⅝ yards of light olive print for border
1½ yards of multicolored focal print for blocks
⅔ yard of light print for blocks
⅔ yard of moss green print for blocks
4⅛ yards of fabric for backing
66" x 78" piece of batting

CUTTING

All cutting dimensions include ¼"-wide seam allowances.

From the multicolored focal print, cut:
10 strips, 4⅞" x 42"

From the deep blue print, cut:
10 strips, 4⅞" x 42"
8 binding strips

From the light print, cut:
7 strips, 2⅞" x 42"; crosscut into 80 squares, 2⅞" x 2⅞".
Cut the squares in half diagonally to make 160 triangles.

From the moss green print, cut:
7 strips, 2⅞" x 42"; crosscut into 80 squares, 2⅞" x 2⅞".
Cut the squares in half diagonally to make 160 triangles.

From the light olive print, cut:
8 border strips, 6½" x 42"

MAKING THE BLOCKS

Press the seam allowances in the direction of the arrows. If there are no arrows, press the seam allowances however you wish.

1. Layer each 4⅞"-wide focal print strip with a 4⅞"-wide deep blue strip, right sides together, to make 10 contrasting strip pairs. From these strip pairs, cut 80 squares, 4⅞" x 4⅞". Cut the layered squares in half diagonally. Do not separate the triangle pairs.

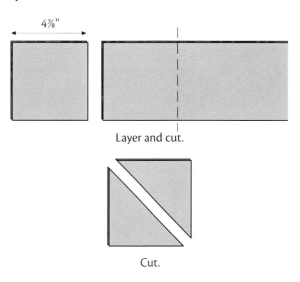

4⅞"

Layer and cut.

Cut.

2. Chain stitch the triangle pairs along the long edges to make 160 half-square-triangle units.

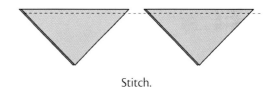

Stitch.

Make 160.

3. Trim the corners from the dark side of 80 units from step 2 and from the light side of the remaining 80 units from step 2. To do so, place the 1⅝" line of your cutting ruler on the diagonal seam of each unit and cut off the piece that extends beyond the ruler. Set the cut-off corners aside to use in another project.

Cut off 80 dark corners.   Cut off 80 light corners.

4. Join the 2⅞" light and moss green triangles to the units from step 3 to make 80 unit A and 80 unit B *exactly* as shown.

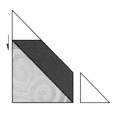

Unit A.
Make 80.

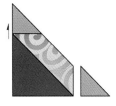

Unit B.
Make 80.

5. Join the units from step 4 to make 80 unit C.

Unit C.
Make 80.

6. Join the units from step 5 *exactly* as shown to make 20 Old Maid's Rambler blocks.

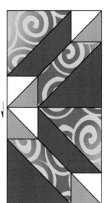

Make 20.

ASSEMBLING AND FINISHING THE QUILT

Basic instructions for borders, backing, and binding begin on page 14.

1. Set the blocks together as shown in the photo on page 120. Press the seam allowances in opposite directions from row to row.
2. Add the border using the 6½"-wide light olive strips.
3. Seam the backing fabric. The seam will run crosswise of the quilt.
4. Layer the quilt top with batting and backing; baste.
5. Hand or machine quilt.
6. Bind the quilt with the deep blue strips.

Purse Seiner

Pieced and quilted by Gen Nestler

Finished block: 12" x 12"
Finished quilt: 50½" x 62½"

MATERIALS

Yardage is based on 42"-wide fabric.

1½ yards of multicolored focal print for border*

1⅛ yards of light print for blocks

12 squares, 12" x 12", of assorted dark prints for blocks. Use a variety of greens, purples, and cranberries.

12 rectangles, 6" x 12", of assorted dark-medium prints for blocks. Use slightly lighter versions of the dark colors above.

12 strips, exactly 2½" wide x 17" long, of assorted light-medium prints for blocks. Use colors that coordinate with the dark and medium prints.

⅝ yard of green print for binding

3½ yards of fabric for backing

57" x 69" piece of batting

Use one of the fabrics you used for the blocks or a completely different fabric.

CUTTING

All cutting dimensions include ¼"-wide seam allowances.

From *each* of the 12 assorted dark-medium prints, cut:

2 strips, 2½" x 12" (24 total); crosscut *12 strips* (one of each fabric) into 48 squares, 2½" x 2½"

From *each* of the 12 assorted dark prints, cut:

1 strip, 4½" x 12" (12 total); crosscut into 48 rectangles, 2½" x 4½"

1 strip, 2½" x 12" (12 total)

2 squares, 2⅞" x 2⅞" (24 total)

From the light print, cut:

2 strips, 2⅞" x 42"; crosscut into 24 squares, 2⅞" x 2⅞"

12 strips, 2½" x 42"; crosscut into:

  96 squares, 2½" x 2½"

  12 rectangles, 2½" x 17"

From the focal print, cut:

6 border strips, 7¾" x 42"

From the green print, cut:

7 binding strips

MAKING THE BLOCKS

For ease of construction, press the seam allowances open.

1. Align 2½" light squares with the left-hand corners of the 2½" x 4½" dark rectangles, right sides together. Draw a diagonal line from corner to corner on each of the light squares as shown and stitch on the lines. Trim to leave ¼"-wide seam allowances; press.

Stitch.   Trim.   Make 48.

2. Align the remaining 2½" light squares with the right-hand corners of the units from step 1, right sides together. Draw, stitch, trim, and press as before.

Stitch.   Trim.   Make 48.

SAVE THE CORNERS

Seam the cut-off corners and use the resulting half-square-triangle units as part of a sawtooth border or for another project.

3. Layer each 2⅞" light square with a 2⅞" dark square, right sides together, to make 24 contrasting pairs. Draw a diagonal line from corner to corner on each light square. Stitch ¼" from each side of the lines. Cut on the drawn lines to make 48 half-square-triangle units.

Layer.   Draw.   Stitch.   Cut.

Make 48.

4. Join the 2½"-wide strips to make 12 dark/dark-medium strip units and 12 light/light-medium strip units as shown. Cut the number of 2½"-wide segments indicated.

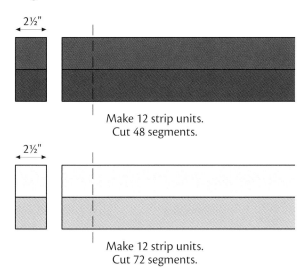

Make 12 strip units.
Cut 48 segments.

Make 12 strip units.
Cut 72 segments.

5. Randomly join the dark/dark-medium strip-unit segments, the 2½" dark-medium squares, and the units from step 3 to make 48 unit A. Orient the strip-unit segments with the dark squares at the top as shown.

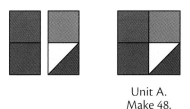

Unit A.
Make 48.

6. Randomly join the units from step 2 and the light/light-medium strip-unit segments to make 48 unit B and 12 unit C.

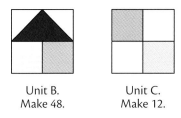

Unit B.
Make 48.

Unit C.
Make 12.

7. Randomly join the units from steps 5 and 6 to make 12 Purse Seiner blocks.

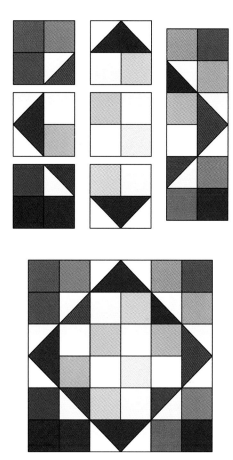

Make 12.

ASSEMBLING AND FINISHING THE QUILT

Basic instructions for borders, backing, and binding begin on page 14.

1. Set the blocks together as shown in the photo on page 123. Press the seam allowances in opposite directions from row to row.
2. Add the border using the 7¾"-wide focal print strips.
3. Seam the backing fabric. The seam will run crosswise of the quilt.
4. Layer the quilt top with batting and backing; baste.
5. Hand or machine quilt.
6. Bind the quilt with the green print strips.

ROLLING NINE PATCH

Pieced and quilted by Carol Parks

Finished block: 7½" x 7½"
Finished quilt: 49½" x 64½"

MATERIALS

Yardage is based on 42"-wide fabric.

3¼ yards of pink print 1 for block backgrounds, setting squares, border, and binding

⅝ yard of pink print 2 for block backgrounds

½ yard of moss green print for blocks

1 fat quarter (18" x 20") of rose print for blocks

1 fat quarter of burgundy print for blocks

2 strips, 2" x 20", of yellow print for blocks

3½ yards of fabric for backing

56" x 71" piece of batting

CUTTING

All cutting dimensions include ¼"-wide seam allowances. **Note:** *You may want to wait until your blocks are pieced before cutting setting squares, in case your blocks measure larger or smaller than the expected 8" x 8" (raw edge to raw edge).*

From the burgundy fat quarter, cut:
8 strips, 2" x 20"

From the rose fat quarter, cut:
8 strips, 2" x 20"

From the moss green print, cut:
4 strips, 3½" x 42"; crosscut into 72 rectangles, 2" x 3½"

From pink print 1, cut:
4 strips, 8" x 42"; crosscut into 17 setting squares, 8" x 8"

8 strips, 2" x 42"; crosscut 6 *strips* into 108 squares, 2" x 2". Leave the remaining strips uncut.

From the *lengthwise grain* of the remaining pink print 1, cut:
4 border strips, 6½" x at least 54"

5 binding strips

From pink print 2, cut:
8 strips, 2" x 42"; crosscut 6 *strips* into 108 squares, 2" x 2". Leave the remaining strips uncut.

USING LEFTOVER FABRIC

Use the leftovers from pink print 1 for another project or as part of a pieced backing.

MAKING THE BLOCKS

Press the seam allowances in the direction of the arrows. If there are no arrows, press the seam allowances however you wish.

1. Join the 2" x 20" burgundy, rose, and yellow strips to make four strip unit A and two strip unit B as shown. Cut the number of 2"-wide segments indicated.

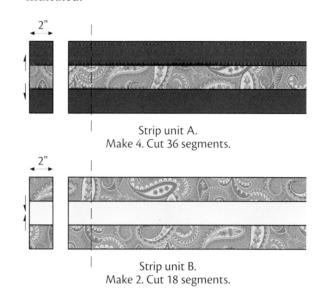

Strip unit A.
Make 4. Cut 36 segments.

Strip unit B.
Make 2. Cut 18 segments.

2. Join the segments from step 1 to make 18 unit C.

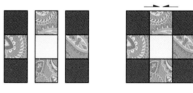

Unit C.
Make 18.

3. Align 2" squares of pink print 1 with the left-hand corners of 36 of the 2" x 3½" moss green rectangles, right sides together. Draw a diagonal line from corner to corner on each pink square as shown and stitch on the lines. Trim to leave ¼"-wide seam allowances; press.

Stitch.   Trim.   Make 36.

4. Align 2" squares of pink print 1 with the right-hand corners of the units from step 3. Draw, stitch, trim, and press as before.

Stitch.   Trim.   Make 36.

5. Join 2" squares of pink print 2 to the units from step 4 to make 36 unit D.

Unit D.
Make 36.

6. Join the 2"-wide strips of pink prints 1 and 2 to make two strip units. From these strip units, cut 36 segments, 2" wide.

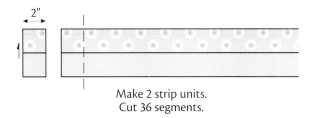

Make 2 strip units.
Cut 36 segments.

7. Repeat steps 3 and 4 with 2" squares of pink print 2 and the remaining 2" x 3½" moss green rectangles. Join the resulting units, the strip-unit segments from step 6, and the remaining 2" squares of pink print 1 to make 36 unit E.

Unit E.
Make 36.

8. Join units C and D to make 18 unit F.

 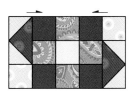

Unit F.
Make 18.

9. Join units E and F to make 18 Rolling Nine Patch blocks.

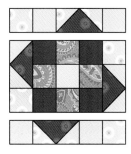 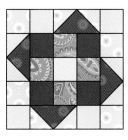

Make 18.

ASSEMBLING AND FINISHING THE QUILT

Basic instructions for borders, backing, and binding begin on page 14.

1. Set the pieced blocks and the 8" setting squares of pink print 1 together as shown in the photo on page 126. Press the seam allowances toward the setting squares.
2. Add the border using the 6½"-wide strips of pink print 1.
3. Seam the backing fabric. The seam will run crosswise of the quilt.
4. Layer the quilt top with batting and backing; baste.
5. Hand or machine quilt.
6. Bind the quilt with the strips of pink print 1.

SALMONBERRY

Pieced and quilted by Elise Rose

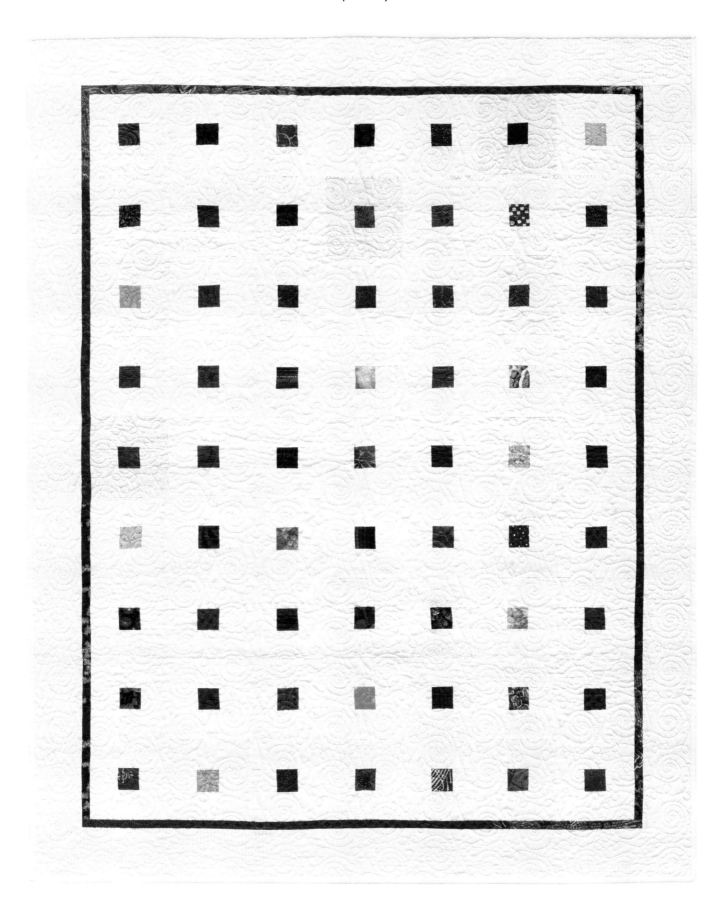

Finished block: 5½" x 5½"
Finished quilt: 46½" x 57½"

MATERIALS

Yardage is based on 42"-wide fabric.

16 fat quarters (18" x 20") of assorted white-on-white prints for blocks, outer border, and binding*

63 squares, 2" x 2", of assorted red, orange, and gold prints for blocks*

5 strips, 1" x 42", of assorted red prints for inner border**

3¼ yards of fabric for backing

53" x 64" piece of batting

Use the same fabric more than once, if you wish.

**Use some of the same fabrics you used for the blocks or completely different fabrics.*

CUTTING

All cutting dimensions include ¼"-wide seam allowances.

From *each* of the 16 white-on-white fat quarters, cut:
1 strip, 6" x 20" (16 total); crosscut into 126 rectangles, 2½" x 6"
1 strip, 2" x 20" (16 total); crosscut into 126 rectangles, 2" x 2½"
1 border strip, 4" x 20" (16 total)
1 binding strip (16 total)

MAKING THE BLOCKS

Press the seam allowances however you wish.
Note: Because there are so many different fabric combinations, strip-piecing methods are not efficient for this quilt. You'll be composing and making one block at a time using just two fabrics in each block.

1. Join matching 2" x 2½" white-on-white rectangles to a red, orange, or gold square to make one unit A.

Unit A.
Make 1.

2. Using rectangles from the same white-on-white fabric as the pieces from step 1, join 2½" x 6" rectangles to the units from step 1 to make one Salmonberry block.

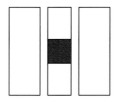 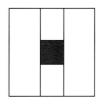

Make 1.

3. Repeat steps 1 and 2 with the remaining squares and rectangles to make a total of 63 blocks.

ASSEMBLING AND FINISHING THE QUILT

Basic instructions for borders, backing, and binding begin on page 14.

1. Set the blocks together as shown in the photo on page 129. Note that every other block is rotated 90º, so the seams are staggered. Press the seam allowances in opposite directions from row to row.

2. Add the inner border, joining the 1"-wide assorted red strips end to end at random to make strips long enough to border the quilt.

3. Add the outer border, joining the 4"-wide white-on-white strips end to end at random to make strips long enough to border the quilt.

4. Seam the backing fabric. The seam will run crosswise of the quilt.

5. Layer the quilt top with batting and backing; baste.

6. Hand or machine quilt.

7. Bind the quilt, joining the white-on-white strips end to end at random to make a strip long enough to bind the quilt.

SIMPLE FLOWER BASKET

Pieced by and quilted by Jean McDaniel

Finished block: 8½" x 8½"
Finished quilt: 43½" x 55½"

MATERIALS

Yardage is based on 42"-wide fabric.

1¼ yards of floral print for outer border and binding

⅞ yard of light print for block backgrounds

4 strips, exactly 6⅞" wide x about 42" long, of assorted green prints for block corners

⅓ yard of brown print 1 for baskets

¼ yard of brown print 2 for inner border

12 rectangles, 3" x 10", of assorted bright prints for "flowers"

3⅛ yards of fabric for backing

50" x 61" piece of batting

CUTTING

All cutting dimensions include ¼"-wide seam allowances.

From the light print, cut:

1 strip, 5⅛" x 42"

2 strips, 4¾" x 42"; crosscut into 24 rectangles, 2⅝" x 4¾"

4 strips, 3" x 42"; crosscut *3 strips* into 12 rectangles, 3" x 10". Leave the remaining strip uncut.

From brown print 1, cut:

1 strip, 5⅛" x 42"

1 strip, 3" x 42"

From *each* of the 4 assorted green strips, cut:

6 squares, 6⅞" x 6⅞" (24 total); cut each square in half diagonally to make 48 triangles

From brown print 2, cut:

5 border strips, 1" x 42"

From the floral print, cut:

6 border strips, 3¾" x 42"

6 binding strips

MAKING THE BLOCKS

Press the seam allowances in the direction of the arrows. If there are no arrows, press the seam allowances however you wish.

1. Layer the 5⅛"-wide light strip with the 5⅛"-wide strip of brown print 1, right sides together, to make a contrasting strip pair. From this strip pair, cut six squares, 5⅛" x 5⅛". Cut the layered squares in half diagonally. Do not separate the triangle pairs.

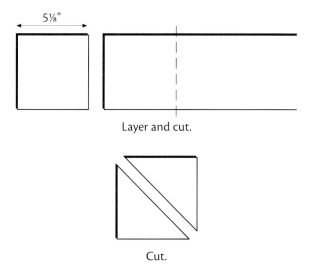

Layer and cut.

Cut.

2. Chain stitch the triangle pairs along the long edges to make 12 large half-square-triangle units.

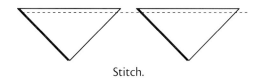

Stitch.

Make 12.

3. Layer the 3"-wide light and brown print 1 strips to make a contrasting strip pair. From this strip pair, cut 12 squares, 3" x 3". Cut the layered squares in half diagonally and chain stitch the triangle pairs along the long edges to make 24 small half-square-triangle units.

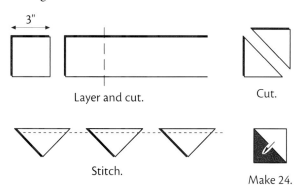

Layer and cut.

Cut.

Stitch.

Make 24.

4. Layer the 3" x 10" light and bright print rectangles to make 12 contrasting strip pairs. From each strip pair, cut three squares, 3" x 3" (36 total). Cut the layered squares in half diagonally and chain stitch the triangle pairs along the long edges to make 72 half-square-triangle units.

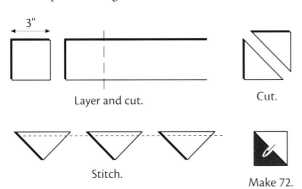

Layer and cut.   Cut.

Stitch.   Make 72.

5. Join 48 of the units from step 4 to make 12 unit A using just two fabrics (the light and one bright print) in each unit.

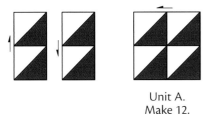

Unit A.
Make 12.

6. Join the units from step 3 and the remaining units from step 4 to make 12 unit B and 12 unit C *exactly* as shown.

Unit B.   Unit C.
Make 12.   Make 12.

7. Join the B and C units and the 2⅝" x 4¾" light rectangles to make 12 unit D and 12 unit E.

Unit D.   Unit E.
Make 12.   Make 12.

8. Join the units you made in the previous steps to make 12 Simple Flower Basket blocks.

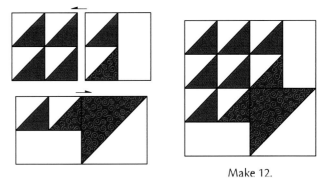

Make 12.

9. Join 6⅞" green triangles to the blocks from step 8 to make 12 units *exactly* as shown (see "Stitching Tips for Square-in-a-Square Units" on page 12).

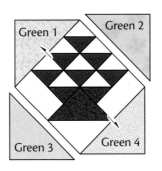

Make 12.

ASSEMBLING AND FINISHING THE QUILT

Basic instructions for borders, backing, and binding begin on page 14.

1. Set the blocks together as shown in the photo on page 131. Press the seam allowances in opposite directions from row to row.
2. Add the inner border using the 1"-wide strips of brown print 2.
3. Add the outer border using the 3¾"-wide floral strips.
4. Seam the backing fabric. The seam will run crosswise of the quilt.
5. Layer the quilt top with batting and backing; baste.
6. Hand or machine quilt.
7. Bind the quilt with the floral strips.

SISTER'S CHOICE

Pieced by Terri Shinn; quilted by Carol Parks; from the collection of Judy Dafoe Hopkins

Finished block: 10" x 10"
Finished quilt: 50" x 70"

MATERIALS

Yardage is based on 42"-wide fabric.

2 yards of red print for blocks

1⅓ yards of multicolored focal print for blocks

⅞ yard of dark multicolored striped fabric for blocks

6 strips, exactly 2⅞" wide x 42" long, of assorted
   medium prints for blocks. Use greens and
   magentas or other colors found in the focal print.

⅝ yard of green plaid for binding

3½ yards of fabric for backing

56" x 76" piece of batting

CUTTING

*All cutting dimensions include ¼"-wide seam
allowances.*

From the red print, cut:

2 strips, 4½" x 42"

6 strips, 2⅞" x 42"

14 strips, 2½" x 42"; crosscut *5 strips* into 76 squares,
   2½" x 2½". Leave the remaining strips uncut.

4 rectangles, 2½" x 4½"

From the multicolored striped fabric, cut:

11 strips, 2½" x 42"; crosscut *5 strips* into 78 squares,
   2½" x 2½". Leave the remaining strips uncut.

From the focal print, cut:

8 strips, 4½" x 42"

1 strip, 2½" x 42"

4 squares, 4½" x 4½"

1 square, 2½" x 2½"

From the green plaid, cut:

7 binding strips

MAKING THE BLOCKS

Press the seam allowances in the direction of the
arrows. If there are no arrows, press the seam
allowances however you wish.

1. Layer each 2⅞"-wide red strip with a 2⅞"-wide
   medium print strip, right sides together, to make
   six contrasting strip pairs. From *each* strip pair,
   cut 12 squares, 2⅞" x 2⅞" (72 total). Cut the layered
   squares in half diagonally. Do not separate the
   triangle pairs.

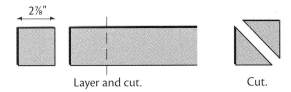

Layer and cut.   Cut.

2. Chain stitch the triangle pairs along the long edges
   to make 144 half-square-triangle units.

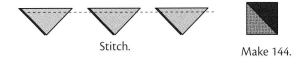

Stitch.   Make 144.

3. Join the units from step 2 and 2½" striped and red
   squares to make 72 unit A. Match the triangles in
   each unit.

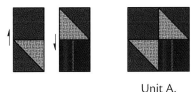

Unit A.
Make 72.

4. Join 2½"-wide striped and red strips to make three strip unit B and one strip unit C. Cut the number of 2½"-wide segments indicated.

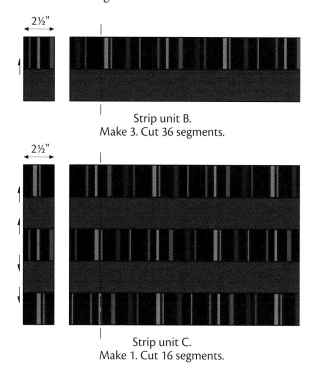

Strip unit B.
Make 3. Cut 36 segments.

Strip unit C.
Make 1. Cut 16 segments.

5. Join six 2½" striped squares and the four remaining 2½" red squares to make two units identical to the segments you cut from strip unit C above, for a total of 18 segments.

6. Join the units from step 3 with the strip-unit segments from steps 4 and 5 to make 18 block A. Match the triangles in each block.

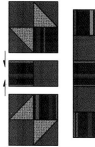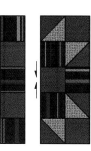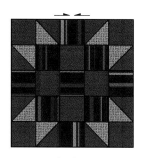

Block A.
Make 18.

7. Join 2½"- and 4½"-wide focal print and red strips to make four strip unit D and one strip unit E. Cut the number of 4½"- and 2½"-wide segments indicated.

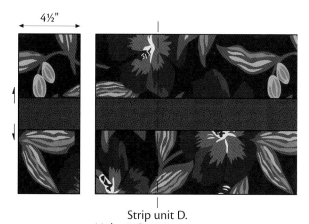

Strip unit D.
Make 4. Cut 32 segments.

Strip unit E.
Make 1. Cut 16 segments.

8. Use the remaining 2½" x 4½" red rectangles, the remaining 4½" focal print squares, and the 2½" focal print square to make two units identical to those you cut from strip unit D and one unit identical to those you cut from strip unit E above.

9. Join the step 7 and step 8 segments to make 17 block B.

Block B.
Make 17.

ASSEMBLING AND FINISHING THE QUILT

Basic instructions for borders, backing, and binding begin on page 14.

1. Set the blocks together as shown, alternating block A and block B. Press the seam allowances toward block B.

2. Seam the backing fabric. The seam will run crosswise of the quilt.

3. Layer the quilt top with batting and backing; baste.

4. Hand or machine quilt.

5. Bind the quilt with the green plaid strips.

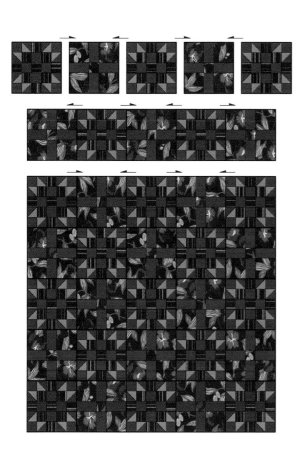

SOARING GULLS

Pieced by Judy Dafoe Hopkins; quilted by Carol Parks

Finished block: 6" x 6"
Finished quilt: 54" x 78"

MATERIALS

Yardage is based on 42"-wide fabric.

1 yard of red print for setting squares

1 yard of blue striped fabric for setting squares

6 strips, exactly 3⅞" x about 42", of assorted light
   prints for blocks

12 rectangles, 12" x 21", of assorted navy prints for
   blocks*

⅔ yard of navy print for binding**

5¼ yards of fabric for backing

60" x 84" piece of batting

Use the same fabric more than once, if you wish.

**Use one of the fabrics you used for the blocks or a
completely different fabric.*

CUTTING

*All cutting dimensions include ¼"-wide seam
allowances.*

**Cut *each* of the 6 assorted light print strips in half
widthwise to make:**
2 strips, 3⅞" x about 21" (12 total)

From *each* of the 12 assorted navy prints, cut:
1 strip, 3⅞" x 21" (12 total)
2 strips, 3½" x 21" (24 total); crosscut *each* strip into 5
   squares, 3½" x 3½" (120 total; you'll use 118)

From the red print, cut:
5 strips, 6½" x 42"; crosscut into 28 setting squares,
   6½" x 6½"

From the blue striped fabric, cut:
5 strips, 6½" x 42"; crosscut into 30 setting squares,
   6½" x 6½"

From the navy print for binding, cut:
8 strips

MAKING THE BLOCKS

Press the seam allowances in the direction of the
arrows. If there are no arrows, press the seam
allowances however you wish.

1. Layer each 3⅞" x about 21" light print strip with a
   3⅞" x 21" navy strip, right sides together, to make
   12 contrasting strip pairs. From these strip pairs,

cut 59 squares, 3⅞" x 3⅞". Cut the layered squares
in half diagonally. Do not separate the triangle
pairs.

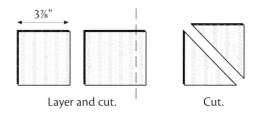

Layer and cut.   Cut.

2. Chain stitch the triangle pairs along the long edges
   to make 118 half-square-triangle units.

Stitch.

Make 118.

3. Join the units from step 2 and the 3½" navy
   squares to make 59 blocks. Make some two-fabric
   blocks (using just one light and one navy print)
   and some three-fabric blocks (using one light and
   two navy prints) as shown.

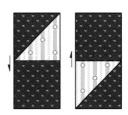

Make 59.

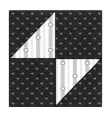
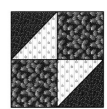

Two-fabric block   Three-fabric block

ASSEMBLING AND FINISHING THE QUILT

Basic instructions for borders, backing, and binding begin on page 14.

1. Join the blocks and the 6½" blue striped and red squares to make seven row A and six row B *exactly* as shown. Note that the pieced blocks are oriented with the plain navy squares at the lower left and upper right, and that the blue stripes all run vertically. Press the seams toward the 6½" squares.

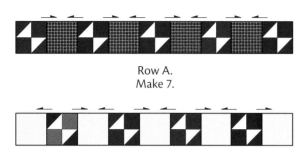

Row A.
Make 7.

Row B.
Make 6.

2. Join the rows as shown.

3. Seam the backing fabric. The seam will run lengthwise of the quilt.
4. Layer the quilt top with batting and backing; baste.
5. Hand or machine quilt.
6. Bind the quilt with the navy strips.

Streak of Lightning

Pieced by Judy Dafoe Hopkins; quilted by Mona Norris

Finished block: 9" x 9"
Finished quilt: 61" x 81"

MATERIALS

Yardage is based on 42"-wide fabric.

3⅓ yards of black print for blocks, side borders, and binding

27 squares, exactly 9⅞" x 9⅞", of assorted Japanese-style prints for blocks*

5⅓ yards of fabric for backing

67" x 87" piece of batting

Use the same fabric more than once, if you wish.

CUTTING

All cutting dimensions include ¼"-wide seam allowances.

From the black print, cut:

7 strips, 9⅞" x 42"; crosscut into 27 squares, 9⅞" x 9⅞"

5 border strips, 4" x 42"

8 binding strips

MAKING THE BLOCKS

For ease of construction, press the seam allowances open.

1. Layer a 9⅞" Japanese-print square and a 9⅞" black square, right sides together, keeping the edges aligned. Draw a diagonal line from corner to corner on the Japanese-print square and stitch ¼" from each side of the line. Cut on the drawn line to make two half-square-triangle units.

Layer.

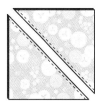

Draw.

Stitch.   Cut.

Make 2.

2. Repeat step 1 with the remaining 9⅞" Japanese-print and black squares for a total of 54 half-square-triangle units.

ASSEMBLING AND FINISHING THE QUILT

Basic instructions for borders, backing, and binding begin on page 14.

1. Set the blocks together as shown. Press the seam allowances in opposite directions from row to row.

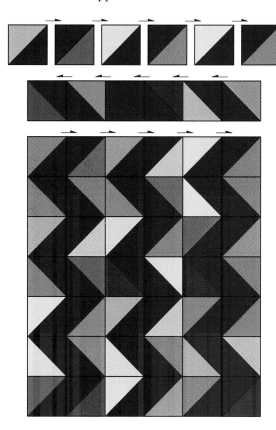

2. Add the side borders using the 4"-wide black print strips.
3. Seam the backing fabric. The seam will run lengthwise of the quilt.
4. Layer the quilt top with batting and backing; baste.
5. Hand or machine quilt.
6. Bind the quilt with the black print strips.

TRISH'S STAR

Pieced by Trish DeLong; quilted by Sue Eickermann; from the collection of Michel Landerman

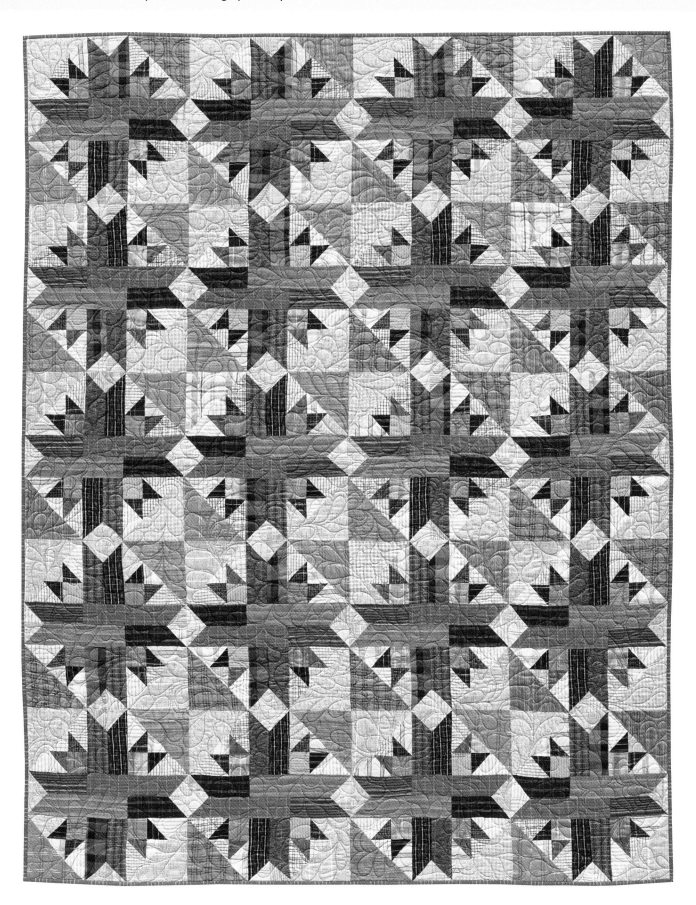

Finished block: 12" x 12"
Finished quilt: 48" x 60"

MATERIALS

Yardage is based on 42"-wide fabric. Use plaids or stripes throughout. All the fabrics listed are for the blocks except as noted.

1 strip, exactly 8" wide x about 42" long, *each* of one dark pink and one tan fabric

1 strip, exactly 5" wide x about 42" long, *each* of one black, one green, one purple, one cherry, one blue, and one teal fabric

8 rectangles, 14" x about 21", of assorted light fabrics*

5 squares, 12" x 12", of assorted light-medium fabrics. Use grays, beiges, and light prints with dark motifs.

5 squares, 12" x 12", of assorted medium fabrics. Use blues, greens, and tans.*

10 strips, exactly 2⅜" wide x about 21" long, of assorted dark fabrics

10 strips, exactly 2" wide x about 18" long, of assorted medium fabrics. At least one of these strips should be cheddar colored.*

½ yard of green fabric for binding

3⅓ yards of fabric for backing

54" x 66" piece of batting

Use some of the same fabrics you used for the 12" x 12" light-medium squares, if you wish.

CUTTING

All cutting dimensions include ¼"-wide seam allowances.

From *each* of the 8 assorted light strips, cut:

2 strips, 2" x 21" (16 total); crosscut into 160 squares, 2" x 2"

5 squares, 4¼" x 4¼" (40 total); cut the squares into quarters diagonally to make 160 triangles. Pin a note that says "4¼" to these triangles.

5 squares, 2⅜" x 2⅜" (40 total); cut the squares in half diagonally to make 80 triangles. Pin a note that says "2⅜" to these triangles.

From *each* of the black, green, purple, cherry, blue, and teal strips, cut:

20 rectangles, 2" x 5" (120 total)

From *each* of the dark pink and tan strips, cut:

20 rectangles, 2" x 8" (40 total)

From *each* of the 10 assorted dark-colored strips, cut:

8 squares, 2⅜" x 2⅜" (80 total); cut the squares in half diagonally to make 160 triangles

From *each* of the 10 assorted medium-colored strips, cut:

8 squares, 2" x 2" (80 total)

From *each* of the 5 assorted light-medium squares and 5 assorted medium-colored squares, cut:

4 squares, 5" x 5" (20 light-medium and 20 medium total); cut the squares in half diagonally to make 80 triangles (40 light-medium and 40 medium)

From the green fabric, cut:

6 binding strips

MAKING THE BLOCKS

Press the seam allowances in the direction of the arrows. To avoid having to twist seam allowances on the back to make the seams butt together properly, you'll press some of the seam allowances open (as indicated by double-headed arrows). If there are no arrows, press the seam allowances however you wish.

1. Align 2" light squares with the right-hand corners of the 2" x 5" black, green, blue, and teal rectangles, right sides together. Draw a diagonal line from corner to corner on each light square as shown and stitch on the lines. Trim to leave ¼" seam allowances; press.

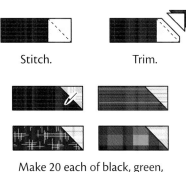

Stitch.   Trim.

Make 20 each of black, green, blue, and teal.

2. Align 2" light squares with the *left-hand* corners of the 2" x 5" purple and cherry rectangles, right sides together. Draw, stitch, and trim as before; press.

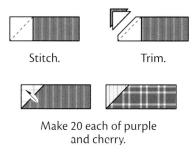

Stitch.   Trim.

Make 20 each of purple and cherry.

3. Join the blue, teal, purple, and cherry units from steps 1 and 2 to make 40 unit A. Use a purple or cherry unit on the left-hand side and a blue or teal unit on the right-hand side throughout.

Unit A.
Make 40.

4. Align the remaining 2" light squares with the *left-hand* corners of the 2" x 8" dark pink and tan rectangles, right sides together. Draw, stitch, trim, and press as before.

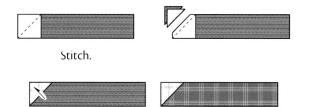

Stitch.

Make 20 each of dark pink and tan.

SAVE THE CORNERS
Seam the cut-off corners and use the resulting half-square-triangle units as part of a sawtooth border or for another project.

5. Join the 2" x 5" black and green units and the 2" x 8" dark pink and tan units to make 20 unit B. Keep the colors in the positions shown throughout.

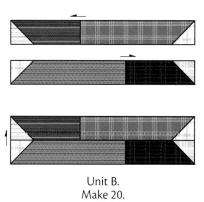

Unit B.
Make 20.

6. Randomly join the 4¼" light triangles, the 2⅜" light and dark triangles, and the 2" medium-colored squares to make 80 unit C. The dark triangles should always be placed in the positions shown.

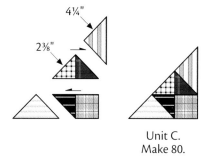

Unit C.
Make 80.

7. Join the 5" light-medium and medium-colored triangles to the C units to make 40 unit D and 40 unit E.

Unit D.
Make 40 using light-medium triangles.

Unit E.
Make 40 using medium triangles.

8. Join the A, B, D, and E units to make 20 Trish's Star blocks. Keep the light-medium triangles at the upper-left and lower-right corners of the blocks throughout.

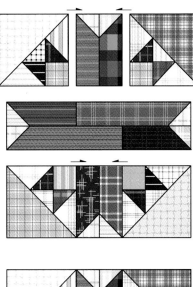

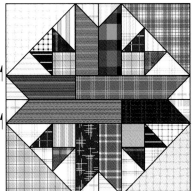

Make 20.

ASSEMBLING AND FINISHING THE QUILT

Basic instructions for borders, backing, and binding begin on page 14.

1. Set the blocks together as shown. Orient all the blocks so the light-medium triangles are at the upper left and lower right. Note that the orientation of the B units is reversed in every other block. Press the seam allowances in opposite directions from row to row.

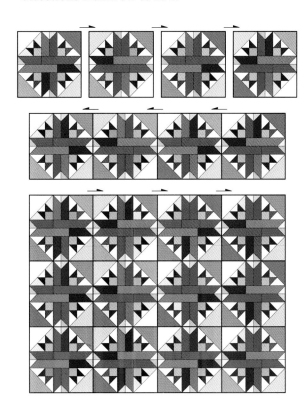

2. Seam the backing fabric. The seam will run crosswise of the quilt.

3. Layer the quilt top with batting and backing; baste.

4. Hand or machine quilt.

5. Bind the quilt with the green strips.

TWILIGHT LANE

Pieced and quilted by Judy Dafoe Hopkins

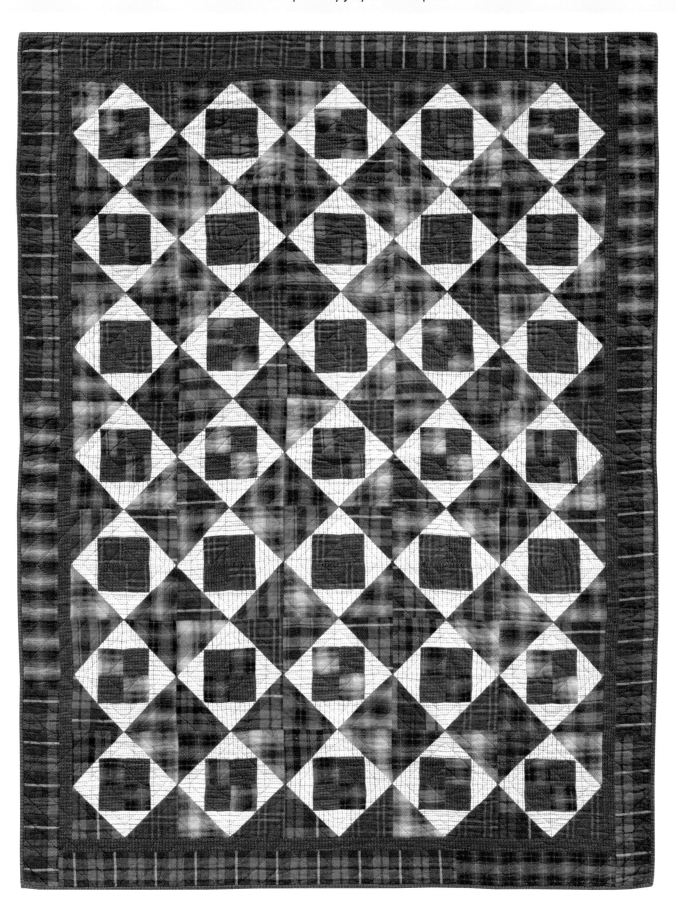

Finished block: 10" x 10"
Finished quilt: 60" x 80"

MATERIALS

Yardage is based on 38"-wide fabric.

⅝ yard *each* of 7 assorted teal plaid flannels for blocks and outer border

1⅔ yards of fuchsia checked flannel for blocks, inner border, and binding

1¼ yards of light checked flannel for block backgrounds

5⅓ yards of fabric for backing

66" x 86" piece of batting

CUTTING

All cutting dimensions include ¼"-wide seam allowances.

From *each* of the 7 assorted teal plaid flannels, cut:

2 strips, 5⅞" x 42" (14 total); crosscut *each* strip into 5 squares, 5⅞" x 5⅞" (70 total). Cut the squares in half diagonally to make 140 triangles.

1 strip, 3" x 42" (7 total)

1 border strip, 4¼" x 42" (7 total)

From the fuchsia checked flannel, cut:

7 strips, 3" x 42"

7 border strips, 1¾" x 42"

8 binding strips

From the light checked flannel, cut:

6 strips, 6¼" x 42"; crosscut into 35 squares, 6¼" x 6¼". Cut the squares into quarters diagonally to make 140 triangles.

USING LEFTOVER FABRIC

Use the leftovers from the teal and fuchsia flannels for another project or as part of a pieced backing.

MAKING THE BLOCKS

Press the seam allowances in the direction of the arrows. If there are no arrows, press the seam allowances however you wish.

1. Join each 3"-wide teal strip to a 3"-wide fuchsia strip to make seven strip units. From *each* strip unit, cut 10 segments, 3" wide (70 total).

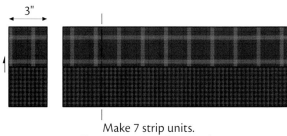

Make 7 strip units.
Cut 10 segments from each.

2. Join the segments from step 1 to make 35 unit A, matching the teal plaids in each unit.

Unit A.
Make 35.

3. Join 6¼" light triangles to the units from step 2 to make 35 unit B (see "Stitching Tips for Square-in-a-Square Units" on page 12).

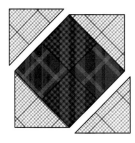 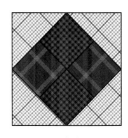

Unit B.
Make 35.

4. Randomly join 5⅞" teal triangles to the units from step 3 to make 35 Twilight Lane blocks.

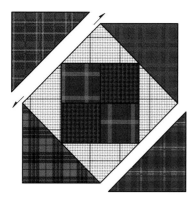

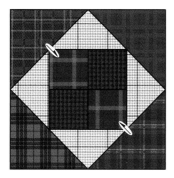

Make 35.

ASSEMBLING AND FINISHING THE QUILT

Basic instructions for borders, backing, and binding begin on page 14.

1. Set the blocks together as shown. Note that the blocks are oriented so the fuchsia squares run on the diagonal from lower left to upper right. Press the seam allowances in opposite directions from row to row.

2. Add the inner border using the 1¾"-wide fuchsia checked strips.
3. Add the outer border, randomly joining the 4¼"-wide teal plaid strips end to end to make strips long enough to border the quilt.
4. Seam the backing fabric. The seam will run lengthwise of the quilt.
5. Layer the quilt top with batting and backing; baste.
6. Hand or machine quilt.
7. Bind the quilt with the fuchsia checked strips.

VIRGINIA REEL

Pieced by Judy Dafoe Hopkins; quilted by Carol Parks

Finished block: 7" x 7"
Finished quilt: 65½" x 79½"

MATERIALS

Yardage is based on 42"-wide fabric.

3 yards of red print for blocks and outer border

2⅛ yards of dark gray print for blocks, inner border, and binding

1⅛ yards of light print 1 for blocks

1⅛ yards of light print 2 for blocks

5¼ yards of fabric for backing

72" x 86" piece of batting

CUTTING

All cutting dimensions include ¼"-wide seam allowances.

From *each* of light prints 1 and 2, the dark gray print, and the red print, cut:

2 strips, 8¼" x 42" (8 total)

1 strip, 4¾" x 42" (4 total); crosscut *each* strip into 8 squares, 4¾" x 4¾" (32 total). Cut the squares into quarters diagonally to make 128 triangles (you'll use 31 of each fabric). Pin a note that says "4¾" to these triangles.

2 strips, 4⅜" x 42" (8 total); crosscut *each* strip into 8 squares, 4⅜" x 4⅜" (64 total). Cut the squares in half diagonally to make 128 triangles (you'll use 31 of each fabric). Pin a note that says "4⅜" to these triangles.

2 strips, 2¼" x 42" (8 total)

From the remaining piece of dark gray print, cut:

7 border strips, 1¾" x 42"

8 binding strips

From the remaining piece of red print, cut:

8 border strips, 7½" x 42"

MAKING THE BLOCKS

Press the seam allowances in the direction of the arrows. If there are no arrows, press the seam allowances however you wish.

1. Join 2¼"-wide strips to make two dark gray and light print 1 strip units and two light print 2 and red strip units as shown. Cut the number of 2¼"-wide segments indicated from each set of strip units.

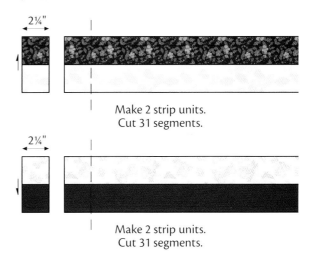

Make 2 strip units.
Cut 31 segments.

Make 2 strip units.
Cut 31 segments.

2. Join the segments from step 1 to make 15 unit A and 16 unit B *exactly* as shown.

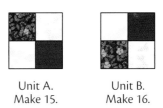

Unit A.
Make 15.

Unit B.
Make 16.

3. Join 4¾" triangles to the step 2 units to make 15 unit C and 16 unit D *exactly* as shown (see "Stitching Tips for Square-in-a-Square Units" on page 12).

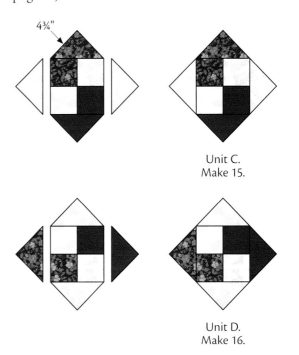

Unit C.
Make 15.

Unit D.
Make 16.

4. Join 4⅜" triangles to the units from step 3 to make 15 unit E and 16 unit F *exactly* as shown.

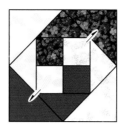

Unit E.
Make 15.

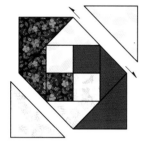

Unit F.
Make 16.

5. Layer each 8¼"-wide strip of light print 1 with an 8¼"-wide strip of light print 2, right sides together, to make two contrasting strip pairs. From these strip pairs, cut six squares, 8¼" x 8¼". Cut the layered squares in half diagonally. Do not separate the triangle pairs.

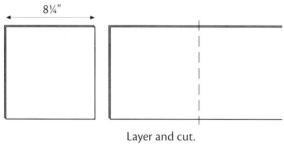

8¼"

Layer and cut.

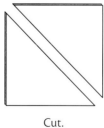

Cut.

6. Chain stitch the triangle pairs along the long edges to make 12 half-square-triangle units.

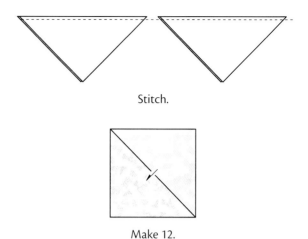

Stitch.

Make 12.

7. Layer the 8¼"-wide dark gray and red strips to make two contrasting strip pairs as before. From these strip pairs, cut 10 squares, 8¼" x 8¼". Cut the layered squares in half diagonally and chain stitch along the long edges to make 20 half-square-triangle units.

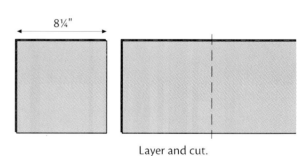

8¼"

Layer and cut.

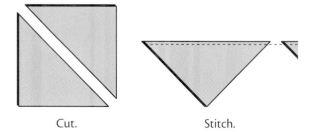

Cut.   Stitch.

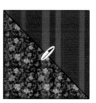

Make 20.

8. Cut the units from steps 6 and 7 in half diagonally as shown. Join the resulting pieces to make 12 unit G and 20 unit H. Note that two divided half-square-triangle units will make two quarter-square-triangle units, but you must "mix and match" the pieces from both units as shown.

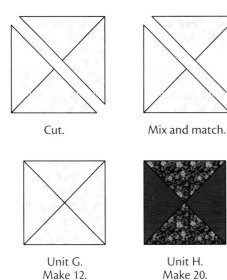

Cut.   Mix and match.

Unit G.   Unit H.
Make 12.   Make 20.

ASSEMBLING AND FINISHING THE QUILT

Basic instructions for borders, backing, and binding begin on page 14.

1. Join the E, F, G, and H units to make three row 1, two row 2, two row 3, and two row 4 *exactly* as shown. Press the seam allowances toward the G and H units.

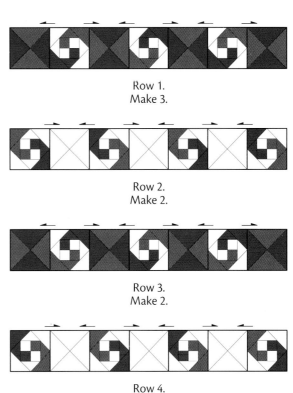

Row 1.
Make 3.

Row 2.
Make 2.

Row 3.
Make 2.

Row 4.
Make 2.

2. Join the block rows in this order, from top to bottom: 1, 2, 3, 4, 1, 2, 3, 4, 1.
3. Add the inner border using the 1¾"-wide dark gray strips.
4. Add the outer border using the 7½"-wide red strips.
5. Seam the backing fabric. The seam will run lengthwise of the quilt.
6. Layer the quilt top with batting and backing; baste.
7. Hand or machine quilt.
8. Bind the quilt with the dark gray strips.

WAGON TRACKS

Pieced by Judy Dafoe Hopkins; quilted by Carol Parks

Finished quilt: 54" x 75"

MATERIALS

Yardage is based on 42"-wide fabric.

4¼ yards of green print for blocks, border, and
   binding

2¼ yards of yellow print for blocks

3⅔ yards of fabric for backing

60" x 81" piece of batting

CUTTING

*All cutting dimensions include ¼"-wide seam
allowances.*

From the yellow print, cut:

2 strips, 4⅜" x 42"

9 strips, 2¼" x 42"

11 strips, 4" x 42"; crosscut 8 *strips* into:

   76 squares, 4" x 4"

   2 squares, 2¼" x 2¼"

Leave the remaining strips uncut.

From the green print, cut:

4 strips, 7½" x 42"; crosscut into:

   38 rectangles, 4" x 7½"

   2 squares, 2¼" x 2¼"

2 strips, 4⅜" x 42"

3 strips, 4" x 42"

9 strips, 2¼" x 42"

From the *lengthwise grain* of the remaining green
print, cut:

4 border strips, 6½" x at least 65"

4 binding strips

USING LEFTOVER FABRIC

Use the leftovers from the yellow and green
prints for another project or as part of a pieced
backing.

MAKING THE BLOCKS

Press the seam allowances in the direction of the
arrows. If there are no arrows, press the seam
allowances however you wish.

1. Join 2¼"- and 4"-wide yellow and green strips to
   make three strip unit A and three strip unit B
   as shown. Cut the number of 2¼"- and 4"-wide
   segments indicated from each set of strip units.

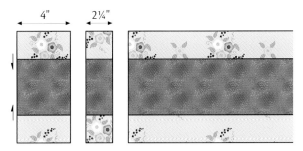

Strip unit A.
Make 3. Cut 7 segments, 4" wide,
and 32 segments, 2¼" wide.

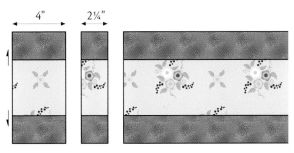

Strip unit B.
Make 3. Cut 8 segments, 4" wide,
and 30 segments, 2¼" wide.

2. Join the segments from step 1 to make 16 unit C,
   eight unit D, and seven unit E.

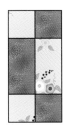
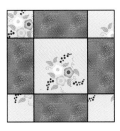

Unit C.
Make 16.

Unit D.
Make 8.

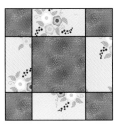

Unit E.
Make 7.

3. Join the remaining 2¼"-wide yellow strips to the remaining 2¼"-wide green strips to make 3 strip unit F. From these strip units, cut 54 segments, 2¼" wide.

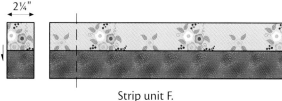

Strip unit F.
Make 3. Cut 54 segments.

4. Join the segments from step 3 and the loose 2¼" squares of yellow and green to make 28 unit G.

Unit G.
Make 28.

5. Layer each 4⅜"-wide yellow strip with a 4⅜"-wide green strip, right sides together, to make two contrasting strip pairs. From these strip pairs, cut 10 squares, 4⅜" x 4⅜". Cut the layered squares in half diagonally. Do not separate the triangle pairs.

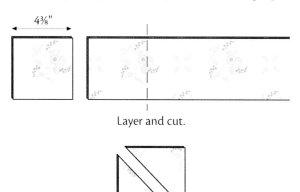

Layer and cut.

Cut.

6. Chain stitch the triangle pairs along the long edges to make 20 unit H.

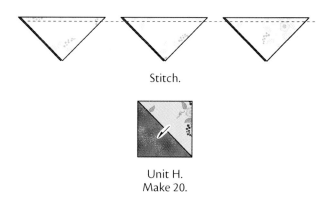

Stitch.

Unit H.
Make 20.

7. Align 4" yellow squares with the left-hand corners of the 4" x 7½" green rectangles. Draw a diagonal line from corner to corner on each of the yellow squares as shown and stitch on the lines. Trim to leave ¼"-wide seam allowances; press.

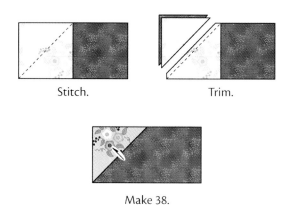

Stitch.   Trim.

Make 38.

8. Align the remaining 2½" yellow squares with the right-hand corners of the units from step 7. Draw, stitch, trim, and press as before to make 38 unit I.

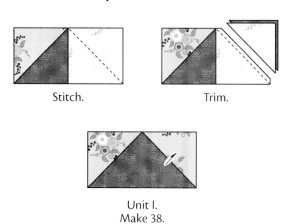

Stitch.   Trim.

Unit I.
Make 38.

SAVE THE CORNERS
Seam the cut-off corners and use the resulting units as part of a sawtooth border or for another project.

ASSEMBLING AND FINISHING THE QUILT
Basic instructions for borders, backing, and binding begin on page 14.

1. Join the units from the preceding section to make two row 1, six row 2, three row 3, and two row 4 *exactly* as shown. Press all the seam allowances away from the triangles.

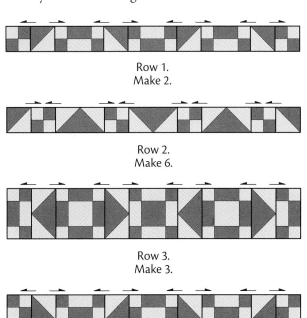

Row 1.
Make 2.

Row 2.
Make 6.

Row 3.
Make 3.

Row 4.
Make 2.

2. Join the block rows in this order from top to bottom: 1, 2, 3, 2 (turned upside down), 4, 2, 3, 2 (turned upside down), 4, 2, 3, 2 (turned upside down), 1 (turned upside down).

3. Add the border using the 6½"-wide green strips.
4. Seam the backing fabric. The seam will run crosswise of the quilt.
5. Layer the quilt top with batting and backing; baste.
6. Hand or machine quilt.
7. Bind the quilt with the green strips.

WHITE HOUSE STEPS

Pieced by Ruth Johnson; quilted by Carol Olsen

Finished quilt: 67½" x 79½"

MATERIALS

Yardage is based on 42"-wide fabric.

3⅛ yards of multicolored focal print for blocks, outer border, and binding

2⅛ yards of gold print for blocks

1 yard of navy print for blocks and inner border

⅞ yard of plum print for blocks and middle border

5¼ yards of fabric for backing

74" x 86" piece of batting

CUTTING

All cutting dimensions include ¼"-wide seam allowances.

From the gold print, cut:

3 strips, 6½" x 42"

4 strips, 5" x 42"

6 strips, 3½" x 42"; crosscut the strips into:
    24 rectangles, 3½" x 6½"
    20 squares, 3½" x 3½"

4 strips, 2" x 42"

From the navy print, cut:

4 strips, 2¾" x 42"

4 strips, 1¼" x 42"

7 border strips, 2" x 42"

From the plum print, cut:

4 strips, 2¾" x 42"

11 strips, 1¼" x 42" (you'll use 7 strips for the middle border)

From the focal print, cut:

5 strips, 3½" x 42"; crosscut into:
    18 rectangles, 3½" x 6½"
    12 rectangles, 3½" x 5"

6 strips, 2" x 42"

8 border strips, 6½" x 42"

8 binding strips

MAKING THE BLOCKS

Press the seam allowances in the direction of the arrows. If there are no arrows, press the seam allowances however you wish.

1. Join 2"-wide gold strips and 1¼"- and 2¾"-wide navy strips to make two strip unit A and two strip unit B. Cut the number of 2"-wide segments indicated from each set of strip units.

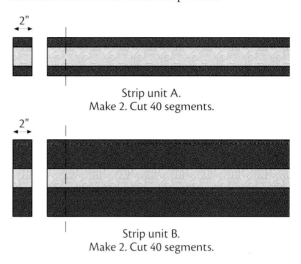

Strip unit A.
Make 2. Cut 40 segments.

Strip unit B.
Make 2. Cut 40 segments.

2. Join the segments from step 1 and the 3½" gold squares to make 20 unit C.

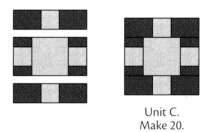

Unit C.
Make 20.

3. Join 5"-wide gold strips and 1¼"- and 2¾"-wide plum strips to make two strip unit D and two strip unit E. Cut the number of 2"-wide segments indicated from each set of strip units.

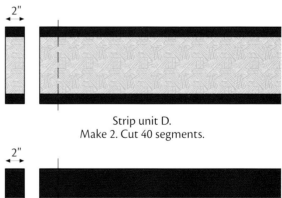

Strip unit D.
Make 2. Cut 40 segments.

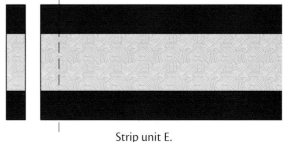

Strip unit E.
Make 2. Cut 40 segments.

4. Join the units from steps 2 and 3 to make 20 unit F.

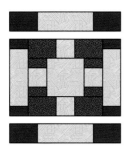

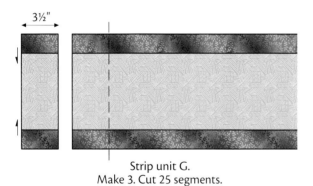

Unit F.
Make 20.

5. Join 6½"-wide gold strips and 2"-wide focal print strips to make three strip unit G. From these strip units, cut 25 segments, 3½" wide.

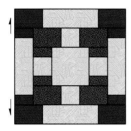

3½"

Strip unit G.
Make 3. Cut 25 segments.

ASSEMBLING AND FINISHING THE QUILT

Basic instructions for borders, backing, and binding begin on page 14.

1. Join the 3½" x 5" and 3½" x 6½" focal print rectangles and the 3½" x 6½" gold rectangles to make six row 1. Press the seam allowances toward the gold rectangles.

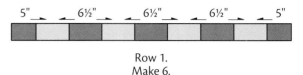

5"   6½"   6½"   6½"   5"

Row 1.
Make 6.

2. Join the F and G units to make five row 2. Press the seam allowances toward the G units.

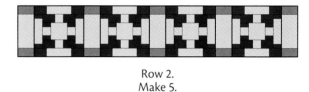

Row 2.
Make 5.

3. Join the rows as shown in the photo on page 158.
4. Add the inner border using the 2"-wide navy strips.
5. Add the middle border using the remaining 1¼"-wide plum strips.
6. Add the outer border using the 6½"-wide focal print strips.
7. Seam the backing fabric. The seam will run lengthwise of the quilt.
8. Layer the quilt top with batting and backing; baste.
9. Hand or machine quilt.
10. Bind the quilt with the focal print strips.

White Pass and Yukon Railroad

Pieced and quilted by Carol Parks

Finished block: 17¼" x 17¼"
Finished quilt: 47" x 64¼"

MATERIALS
Yardage is based on 42"-wide fabric.

2⅝ yards of gray print for blocks, inner and outer borders, and binding

1¼ yards of turquoise print for blocks and middle border

1⅓ yards of light print for block backgrounds

3¼ yards of fabric for backing

53" x 71" piece of batting

CUTTING
All cutting dimensions include ¼"-wide seam allowances.

From the light print, cut:
2 strips, 12" x 42", crosscut each strip into:
20 rectangles, 1⅛" x 12" (40 total)
8 rectangles, 1¾" x 12" (16 total)
5 strips, 3¾" x 42", crosscut into 48 squares, 3¾" x 3¾". Cut the squares in half diagonally to make 96 triangles.

From the turquoise print, cut:
1 strip, 12" x 42"; crosscut into 24 rectangles, 1⅛" x 12"
1 strip, 8⅝" x 42"; crosscut into 24 rectangles, 1⅛" x 8⅝". From the remaining piece of this strip, cut 2 squares, 3¾" x 3¾".
1 strip, 3¾" x 42"; crosscut into 10 squares, 3¾" x 3¾". Add the squares you cut above to this pile, for a total of 12 squares. Cut the squares in half diagonally to make 24 triangles.
2 strips, 3⅜" x 42"; crosscut into 24 squares, 3⅜" x 3⅜"

From the remaining turquoise print, cut:
5 border strips, 1½" x 42"

From the gray print, cut:
1 strip, 12" x 42"; crosscut into 24 rectangles, 1⅛" x 12"
1 strip, 8⅝" x 42"; crosscut into 24 rectangles, 1⅛" x 8⅝". From the remaining piece of this strip, cut 2 squares, 3¾" x 3¾".
1 strip, 3¾" x 42"; crosscut into 10 squares, 3¾" x 3¾". Add the squares you cut above to this pile, for a total of 12 squares. Cut the squares in half diagonally to make 24 triangles.
2 strips, 3⅜" x 42"; crosscut into 24 squares, 3⅜" x 3⅜"

From the remaining gray print, cut:
5 border strips, 1½" x 42"
6 border strips, 4¾" x 42"
6 binding strips

MAKING THE BLOCKS
Press the seam allowances in the direction of the arrows. To avoid having to twist seam allowances on the back to make the seams butt together properly, you'll press some of the seam allowances open (as indicated by double-headed arrows). If there are no arrows, press the seam allowances however you wish.

1. Join the 1⅛" x 12" light, turquoise, and gray rectangles to make four light-and-turquoise strip units and four light-and-gray strip units as shown. Each strip unit uses six colored strips and five light strips.

Make 4.

Make 4.

2. Add 1¾" x 12" light rectangles to the tops and bottoms of each unit from step 1, *and then* cut the number of 3⅜"-wide segments indicated from each set of strip units.

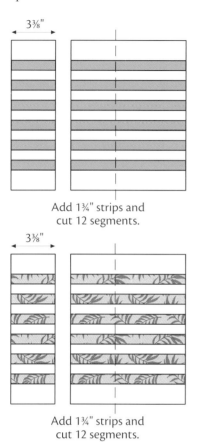

Add 1¾" strips and cut 12 segments.

Add 1¾" strips and cut 12 segments.

3. Center and join 1⅛" x 8⅝" turquoise and gray rectangles to the long edges of the segments from step 2 to make 12 unit A and 12 unit B. Trim the excess light fabric even with the ends of the 8⅝" strips as shown.

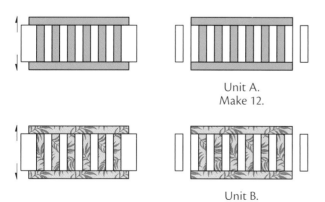

Unit A.
Make 12.

Unit B.
Make 12.

4. Join the 3⅜" turquoise and gray squares and the 3¾" light triangles to make 24 unit C and 24 unit D.

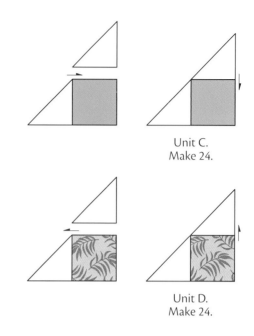

Unit C.
Make 24.

Unit D.
Make 24.

5. Join the units from steps 3 and 4 to make 12 unit E and 12 unit F.

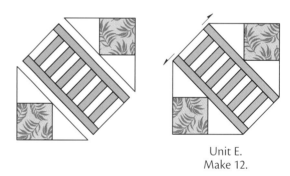

Unit E.
Make 12.

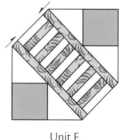

Unit F.
Make 12.

6. Add 3¾" turquoise and gray triangles to the corners of the units from step 5 to make 12 unit G and 12 unit H.

 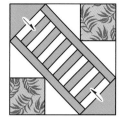 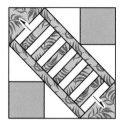

Unit G.
Make 12.

Unit H.
Make 12.

7. Join the units from step 6 to make six White Pass and Yukon Railroad blocks.

Make 6.

ASSEMBLING AND FINISHING THE QUILT

Basic instructions for borders, backing, and binding begin on page 14.

1. Set the blocks together as shown. Note that the blocks are oriented so the turquoise "rails" are at the upper left and lower right. Press the seam allowances in opposite directions from row to row.

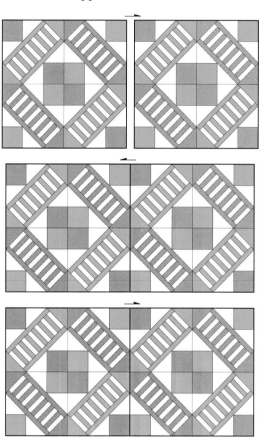

2. Add the inner border using the 1½"-wide gray strips.
3. Add the middle border using the 1½"-wide turquoise strips.
4. Add the outer border using the 4¾"-wide gray strips.
5. Seam the backing fabric. The seam will run crosswise of the quilt.
6. Layer the quilt top with batting and backing; baste.
7. Hand or machine quilt.
8. Bind the quilt with the gray strips.

WRENCH

Pieced and quilted by Julie Wilkinson Kimberlin

Finished block: 8¾" x 8¾"

Finished quilt: 54¼" x 74¼"

MATERIALS

Yardage is based on 42"-wide fabric.

1½ yards of red striped fabric for border

1½ yards of navy print for sashing strips and binding

⅛ yard of red print for sashing posts

24 rectangles, 8" x 13", of assorted cream and tan prints for blocks*

24 rectangles, 8" x 11", of assorted red and blue prints for blocks*

3¾ yards of fabric for backing

61" x 81" piece of batting

Use the same fabric more than once, if you wish.

CUTTING

All cutting dimensions include ¼"-wide seam allowances. Note: You may want to wait until your blocks are pieced before cutting sashing strips, in case your blocks measure larger or smaller than the expected 9¼" x 9¼" (raw edge to raw edge).

From *each* of the 24 assorted cream and tan prints, cut:

1 strip, 2¼" x 13" (24 total); from one end of *each* strip, cut 1 square, 2¼" x 2¼" (24 squares total)

1 rectangle, 4⅜" x 11" (24 total)

From *each* of the 24 assorted red and blue prints, cut:

1 strip, 2¼" x 11" (24 total)

1 rectangle, 4⅜" x 11" (24 total)

From the navy print, cut:

3 strips, 9¼" x 42"; crosscut into 58 sashing strips, 1¾" x 9¼"

7 binding strips

From the red print, cut:

2 strips, 1¾" x 42"; crosscut into 35 sashing squares, 1¾" x 1¾"

From the red striped fabric, cut:

7 border strips, 7" x 42"

MAKING THE BLOCKS

Press the seam allowances in the direction of the arrows. If there are no arrows, press the seam allowances however you wish. **Note:** You'll be composing and making one block at a time using just two fabrics in each block. The cream or tan fabric is referred to as "light" and the red or blue fabric is referred to as "dark."

1. Choose one 2¼"-wide light strip and one 2¼"-wide dark strip that go well together. Join these strips to make a strip unit, keeping one end even. From this strip unit, cut four segments, 2¼" wide.

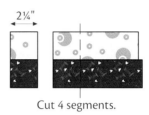

Cut 4 segments.

2. Using the same two fabrics as in step 1, layer the 4⅜" x 11" light and dark strips, right sides together, to make a contrasting strip pair. From this strip pair, cut two squares, 4⅜" x 4⅜". Cut the layered squares in half diagonally. Do not separate the triangle pairs.

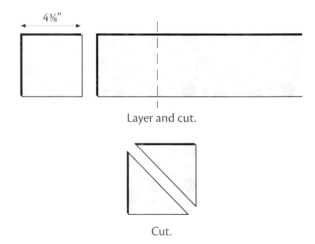

Layer and cut.

Cut.

3. Chain stitch the triangle pairs along the long edges to make four half-square-triangle units.

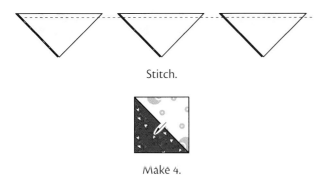

Stitch.

Make 4.

4. Join the segments from step 1, the units from step 3, and a matching 2¼" light square to make one Wrench block.

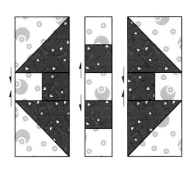

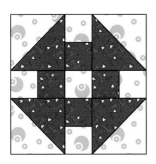

Make 1.

5. Repeat steps 1–4 with the remaining light and dark prints to make a total of 24 blocks.

ASSEMBLING AND FINISHING THE QUILT

Basic instructions for borders, backing, and binding begin on page 14.

1. Join the blocks and 30 of the 1¾" x 9¼" navy sashing strips to make six block rows. Press the seam allowances toward the sashing.

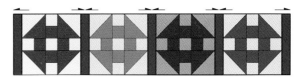

Make 6 block rows.

2. Join the remaining navy sashing strips and the 1¾" red sashing squares to make seven sashing rows. Press the seam allowances toward the navy rectangles.

Make 7 sashing rows.

3. Set the block rows and the sashing rows together as shown in the photo on page 165.
4. Add the border using the 7"-wide red striped strips.
5. Seam the backing fabric. The seam will run crosswise of the quilt.
6. Layer the quilt top with batting and backing; baste.
7. Hand or machine quilt.
8. Bind the quilt with the navy strips.

MEET THE QUILTMAKERS

I asked the people who pieced these beautiful quilts to tell you a little about themselves. Here's what they had to say.

Willa Allison, Post Falls, Idaho

My mother-in-law sent me a book called *Primarily Patchwork* in 1982. I really hadn't thought much about quilting before, but once I read that book, that was it! I tried a few small projects on my own, and then decided I needed to take a class. Over the years I have learned that the projects in which you invest the most of yourself turn out to be the most wonderful. That's why I love hand quilting so much. Joy comes from giving quilts, a part of yourself, to those you love.

Kristi Castanette, Lake Oswego, Oregon

I started sewing when I was 10 and learned about patchwork and quilting from a magazine when I was in my twenties. After I got married and had children, I dabbled in quilting when time permitted, making baby quilts and patchwork items for craft bazaars. Today, quilting is my favorite pastime. I love the beautiful fabrics, the endless supply of fabulous patterns, and the feelings of creativity and relaxation that come with making a quilt. I also enjoy and appreciate the lasting friendships I've made through the small quilt groups and the quilt guild to which I belong.

Susan Baxter, Tigard, Oregon

I have spent most of my life with a needle in my hand, first at my grandmother's side and later as the owner of Fanno Creek Calicos in Tigard, Oregon. Now I host Thimbleberries as a Block of the Month program and do long-arm machine quilting for others.

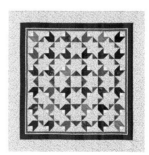

Lisa Cavanaugh, Hillsboro, Oregon

I live in Hillsboro, Oregon, with my husband, John, our son, Matthew, and our family's yellow Lab, Lucy. I started quilting in 1999 when I saw a quilt that my sister-in-law was working on and became intrigued by the pattern. I've been quilting for more than a decade now and frame quilting for more than two years. My favorite parts of the process are planning a project, choosing fabric, and doing the quilting. I have a mid-arm quilting business, and recently a joint-project quilt received first place at the Oregon State Fair.

Anita Daggett, Beaverton, Oregon

I live in Beaverton, Oregon, with my husband, Ken. I have been quilting for 40 years, and I still thrive on the challenge of choosing fabrics to complement a design. Besides quilting, I enjoy tatting, embroidery, knitting, and beadwork.

Trish DeLong, Fairbanks, Alaska

Trish's closest friend, Michel Landerman, tells us: "Trish began her quilting career over 25 years ago by taking a class at a fabric shop and never looking back! Her enthusiasm led her on frequent quilt journeys up and down the west coast, taking classes from all the top teachers and learning numerous skills. Trish loved color, fabric, and traditional patterns, and she soon developed her own distinct style. Her piecing skills were impeccable, and she could spend hours working on intricate patterns. Trish was a natural teacher and soon discovered she loved sharing her talents with others. She taught machine-piecing skills to hundreds of students, who also developed her excitement about quilting. Trish's quilts have appeared in numerous books and shows.

"Trish's love of quilting was surpassed only by her love for her husband and two daughters."

Marilyn Fisher, Hillsboro, Oregon

My mother didn't sew; she embroidered. My aunt and my grandmother embroidered, knitted, crocheted, and quilted. My Aunt Marian taught me English paper piecing when I was 13. My first quilt was a combination of paper piecing and appliqué; I still have that quilt.

I've been quilting now for more than 40 years—longer than I've been married. I enjoy quilting for the color and the friendships it brings into my life. I have a very understanding husband who finally discovered exactly how much fabric I have, and who doesn't care as long as it makes me happy.

Judy Forrest, Juneau, Alaska

For me, quilting has been a husband-and-wife affair. I moved to Juneau, Alaska, in 1958. During my Juneau years the number of quilt stores has ranged from zero to three; there is yet to be any road out of town. The problem of no quilt stores and no roads was resolved by my husband driving me from quilt store to quilt store throughout the western United States on our vacations. He could remember where we'd been and where to go, and I knew what I wanted when I got there. Many of my quilts, including the one in this book, are the result of these trips.

Bev Fugazzi, Beaverton, Oregon

My mom taught me embroidery and knitting, and my dad taught me to hand sew. He also bought me my first sewing machine—a $50 refurbished Kenmore that I still have.

I have always loved quilts, but my first quilted pillow cover was so awful, I was happy when it got stained and had to be thrown away. I met Judy Hopkins through my husband, who drove an airport shuttle. One day he said that Judy would be riding, and asked if I would like to come along and meet her. Judy asked if I had done much quilting; I replied that I mostly just read quilting books. She said, "I know this little quilt shop . . ." My first block-of-the-month was a paper-pieced American Beauty block. After that, I knew I could make anything!

Janet Strait Gorton, Anchorage, Alaska

Alaska has been my home for more than 44 years. I now split my time between Alaska and our great three grandsons, Satcher, Trice, and Mason, and the sunny Southeast.

I taught myself to sew and made baby clothes and the occasional outfit, but I came to quilting with a vengeance! It has inspired some previously untapped creativity within me, and has provided me with friends for life and countless great memories. I have led quilting classes, and have taught the children of friends and even my nephew how to quilt. The joys and sorrows of life are stitched into each and every quilt.

Michelle Hall, Aloha, Oregon

I have a background in art, mechanical drafting, and technical writing. My two biggest passions are quilting and dogs. I started quilting in the early 1990s. I'm sad to say that I haven't done any quilting for some time. For the last five years, my time has literally "gone to the dogs." I train and show two of my dogs in agility, with little side excursions into obedience, carting, and herding. My third dog occasionally does tracking and nose work. I do have several quilt projects that I would like to finish, and hope to get to them someday!

Ruth Johnson, Juneau, Alaska

I started piecing in the '70s but didn't make my first complete quilt until 1982. Quilting has been a passion since that first quilt, but it has to compete with cycling as a main interest. Sometimes having two interests can lead to interesting choices. Once, on a long bike tour, I couldn't resist stopping by a quilt shop—and then had to figure out where to stash two yards of fabric on my road bike. As any true quilter knows, when it comes to fabric, one can always find a way!

Julie Kimberlin, Placerville, California

I'm a self-taught needle artist who began sewing at age 13 (I'm still using the same machine). I graduated from the University of Washington in 1971 with a B.A. in Textiles, Clothing and Art. While I've never used my "specialty," the learning never ends. I began what I thought was a "granny thing"—quilting—in 1985. I'm not sure what triggered the interest that became the disease, but color is my "hook." My work has received many awards, including two national ribbons. I've been published about two dozen times, and it's a thrill each time. I've been married nearly 30 years and my only daughter is currently in graduate school at the University of Washington.

Martha Morris, Juneau, Alaska

Quilts bring joy, challenge, and beauty into my life. I find it a pleasure to make something to fit into the lives of those I love. I enjoy many styles of quilts, and love playing with color and watching the design develop. Frequently, it's a surprise!

Quilting has brought me so many friendships. My children are grown and quilting has filled the time I used to spend on their activities. Of course grandchildren need time now, but I've got them quilting when time permits—the best of both worlds. I live on the edge of Auke Bay with ocean in front and forest behind. I feel so blessed.

Jean McDaniel, Lebanon, Oregon

A lifelong fascination with fabrics, their textures and colors led me down the path to quilting. I made my first quilt in 1982 and have enjoyed quiltmaking ever since. I appreciate all quilts, traditional or contemporary. Once I began machine quilting, I discovered a new passion; I started a professional long-arm quilting business in 2004. Simple or sublime, combining piecing or appliqué with machine quilting is an artistic endeavor that provides perpetual enjoyment for me. See more of my work at www.santiamriverquilts.com.

Dee Morrow, Sacramento, California

Known as Belle Fisher in my other life, I am the wandering Gypsy quilter, packing my caravan of fabric and unfinished projects wherever I go. Together with a circulating load of books and my trusty guitar, from Pennsylvania to Indonesia to Alaska to Trinidad (with stops in between), I look for and find inspiration all around.

Gen Nestler, Juneau, Alaska

Now a retired nurse, I started quilting about 25 years ago. Before I took classes or read quilting books, I used flannel from my long nightgown for squares and part of an old quilted mattress pad for potholders. Nowadays I actually go to quilt stores and know what products to get! I love taking classes, going to retreats, and visiting quilt shops whenever I travel. I like a variety of quilt styles and techniques and love to learn more. Scrap quilts are my current favorite—the more fabrics, the better!

Anne Richardson, Anchorage, Alaska

When I was in high school I realized I wanted to spend my life making art. I pursued that dream intermittently until moving to Alaska, when I was able to concentrate more intensely on creative things. When I lived in Sitka, I painted in oils. I focused on pottery in my early Anchorage years; when a wrist injury requiring surgery put an end to my pottery making, I turned to quiltmaking. I especially love the process of selecting and combining fabrics.

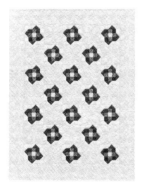

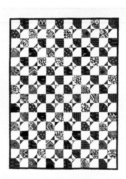

Carol Parks, Beaverton, Oregon

I started quilting after receiving a quilted table runner as a Christmas gift from my parents in 1996. I took my first quilting class in 1997 and was instantly hooked. When I saw my first long-arm quilting machine, I knew I had to have one. My first machine was delivered in January of 2000, and I was off and quilting. Since then I've upgraded three times. I love my machine, and on most days I love my work. Every day I feel blessed because my hobby is my job.

Elise Rose, Anchorage, Alaska

I started quilting when I had young children and needed an activity that I could pick up easily and that was a "dry mess." I didn't know about the lint problem! I love exotic fabrics, particularly Japanese and African fabrics, and am currently fascinated by South American designs. The children have grown, but quilting, especially experimenting with new patterns, continues.

Terri Shinn, Snohomish, Washingnton

I've been a quilter for more than 30 years. The journey of auditioning, tackling new techniques, discovery, and play has been exciting. I continue to experiment with texture, color, and different ways of "torturing" fabric. It's been fun being in so many books and winning awards, but most rewarding is entertaining myself and striving to master new things.

Blanche Smith, Lesterville, Missouri

Her niece Jeanie Smith remembers: "When I met her I was about 12 years old. She and my uncle owned a little store in a small town in Missouri. While working in the store she would piece quilts, especially in the winter. She saw that I was interested and showed me a bunch of quilt tops and told me to pick one out. It was a fan quilt. She gave it to me and I still have it. The Lady of the Lake quilt was a high school graduation present.

"She is the reason I quilt."

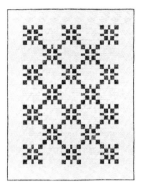

George Taylor, Anchorage, Alaska

I may have been destined to become a quiltmaker: my mother taught me, at age 14, to sew my own shirts! I came to Alaska at the age of nine and, during high school in Kenai and college in Wyoming, developed an interest in knitting, needlepoint, and cross-stitching. I made my first quilt, a flour-sack pinwheel, in 1965.

I've taken many classes and workshops, have exhibited nationally, and have won blue ribbons and Best of Show awards from the Wyoming and Alaska State Fairs. A retired draftsman, I'm an enthusiastic member of the Anchorage Log Cabin Quilters.

Juli Thompson, Banks, Oregon

A descendant of several generations of quiltmakers, I have fond memories of learning to sew craft projects on my mother's New Home machine as a young girl. I fell in love with quilting after visiting my local quilt shop nearly eight years ago. I enjoy making quilts for family and friends, learning new techniques, and being a part of the quilting community. I live in Banks, Oregon, with Erik, my husband of 14 years, and our beloved four-year-old son, Benjamin. There is never enough time in the day for all the projects waiting for me in my quilt room!

Tina Tomsen, Anchorage, Alaska

Coming from a family of crafters and already facile in many other types of handwork, I took up quilting when my oldest child let go of my knee. Though my job in medicine remains consuming, the children are leaving home, and my play with color and pattern continues to evolve. These days, my best works are made from the scraps of a previous pieced quilt project, which then pulls additional fabrics into the mix. Sometimes I even let myself use the scraps *first* (so wild, so daring!), after cutting out a project.

Rhoda Walker, Juneau, Alaska

I live in Juneau, Alaska. I learned to quilt more than 20 years ago, while living in Montana. My love of quilting has grown over the years, and I share this love by teaching individuals in my home and by making donation quilts. My current passion is creating original quilts and quilted wearable-art jackets. Freehand quilting is very relaxing and a form of meditation for me, so it's my favorite part of the quiltmaking process.

Cherrie VanElverdinghe, Dallas, Oregon

I've moved 55 times and lived in 10 states (no, I'm not military!), pretty remarkable considering that I have spent 11½ years at my last address. I have been sewing since I was 11, and quilting since I was 13. My husband and I have three children, two of them at home. We live on a small farm with cows, goats, ducks, and chickens. Between the critters and the kids, we don't need TV.

Judy Hopkins comes from a family of quilters; her grandmother, her mother, and her aunt all made quilts. She started pursuing a career in quilting after being named Alaska state winner of the Great American Quilt Contest in 1986. Since then, she's made dozens of quilts, taught and exhibited across the United States and Canada, created a multitude of mystery quilt patterns, designed a collection of sterling silver jewelry for quilters, and written or co-written 19 pattern and design books, including *101 Fabulous Rotary Cut Quilts* (with Nancy J. Martin, Martingale & Company, 1998) and *501 Rotary-Cut Quilt Blocks* (Martingale & Company, 2008).

Judy loves pattern—patterned fabrics, patterned surfaces—and feels she does her best work when she's working with a dozen or more fabrics in a single quilt, rather than just a few. While she enjoys the process of hand quilting, she feels she's "done" when she's finished piecing a top: "I don't feel guilty about the tops that never get quilted. Maybe someone will enjoy finishing them later." Judy offers this advice to quilters: "Make as many quilts as you can. If you piece at least 12 quilts a year, you're bound to get a few really good ones. The rest you can use for backs."

Judy and her husband, Bill, live in Juneau, Alaska, in a quirky old house with a great harbor view. They enjoy their friends and family and spend as much time as they can with their five interesting grandchildren, who live in Alaska and Oregon.

THERE'S MORE ONLINE!

Visit www.JudyHopkinsquilt.com to learn more about Judy's books, mystery quilt patterns, and line of gorgeous sterling silver jewelry.

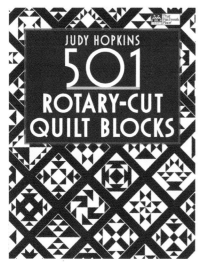
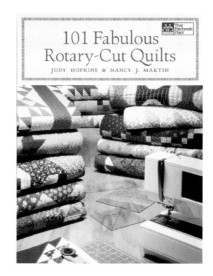

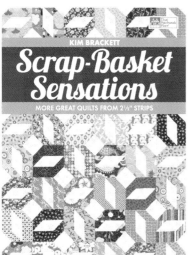
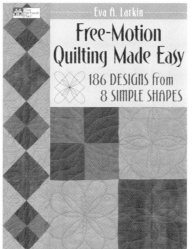
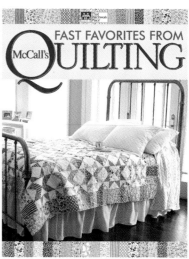
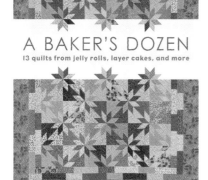